Think About It

A Self Coaching Workbook for Nurturing Personal Leadership Style

Mike Malinchok

AuthorHouse™
1663 Liberty Drive
Bloomington, IN 47403
www.authorhouse.com
Phone: 1-800-839-8640

Published by AuthorHouse 7/26/2013

ISBN: 978-1-4817-7790-2 (sc)
ISBN: 978-1-4817-7827-5 (e)

Library of Congress Control Number: 2013912685

authorHOUSE®

Introduction

'So often times it happens that we live our lives in chains
And we never even know we have the key.'
from

"Already Gone" by the Eagles

Effective Personal Leadership Style manifests for us all when we can clearly and concisely answer these two questions:

Who am I?
What do I do?

The most powerful roadblocks to peak effectiveness for many leaders tend to manifest when they are not perfectly clear in how to answer these two questions. Often times, we get trapped in past models of behavior that were successful for a while in our career path, however, if we're not attentive to progressing times they become the 'chains' that hold us back.

In my career, I have crossed paths with several leadership mentors who didn't all answer these two questions in the same way, but rather had a unique and deeply personal style that drew me to watch, follow, and learn from them.

Three specific ones who come to mind demonstrate the power of <u>personal </u>leadership style that is borne out of proven strengths and passions:

Early in my career, I was fortunate to have worked for a sales manager whose intellect both inspired and intimidated me. She had a full grasp of the business objectives our company had and never lost sight of them in our shared quest to hit our sales quotas. Her ability to quickly evaluate opportunities and make sound decisions on whether or not to pursue them was nothing short of astonishing.

Leading a group of highly competitive sales folks whose primary mission was to make their quotas often times put her business decisions into direct conflict with hitting personal quotas. However, year after year, her team consistently hit the organizational quotas and we were able to proudly enjoy the reputation within the company of putting quality, profitable business on the books.

So, because we all grew to trust and rely on her business acumen, there was rarely a disagreement or push back to the decisions she made. Her answers to the two questions above might have been:

> *1. I am a smart sales leader.*
> *2. I deliver the right clients at the right time for the right price.*

Further along in my career, I worked for an entrepreneur who had a very clear vision for his company that he manifested with astonishing speed. While company longevity and personal legacy were often considered important criteria for the kind of company I wanted to work for, this owner shared with me a rather startling vision for me to consume in the first two minutes of meeting him: 'Within 6 months, this company will be positioned for acquisition, at which time each employee will benefit financially and move on to the next phase of their career each a little bit wealthier.' It shook my conservative East-Coast career path mentality to the core and intrigued me enough to accept the job and open myself up to a new way of thinking.

As I observed and supported the decisions he made for the company, it was clear that he was committed to carrying out his vision…and he made it happen…ahead of schedule. His answers to the two questions above might have been:

> *1. I am a business opportunist.*
> *2. I create timely companies that sell quickly and profitably.*

A third example of effective personal leadership style that I have been fortunate enough to experience was with a company founder who I would categorize as a dreamer. In my time working for this leader, there was a consistency about his style that was the solid foundation and the guiding light during the most challenging times of my employment with him. When asked his vision for the company and its products, he unabashedly would state ' the company name will be a part of the standard industry lexicon and the products will be available on the desktop of everyone in the world employed in our field'.

And, within a few years, it happened. His answers to the two questions above might have been:

I am a visionary.
I change business as usual and redefine the 'norm'.

All three could be objectively defined as highly successful in their positions. To me, what made them compelling leadership mentors was how seamlessly they blended their own personal strengths and talents into the fabric that was the time and place in which our paths crossed.

What makes them any different from you or me? Organically, there is no difference.

Here's what I came to realize might be different:

They've done the internal work to recognize and embrace their own strengths and attributes. They capitalize on them and, with remarkable hubris, lead with them in every situation they encounter.

In relation to their professional role, they know <u>exactly</u> who they are and they know <u>exactly</u> what they do.

My purpose in writing *Think About It* was to provide my clients with a set of self-coaching tools (or 'keys to the chains') to help find and nurture their own answers to the questions: Who am I? and What do I do?

Sometimes life circumstances force us to scramble in understanding our unique personal value as we move through challenging events like a job layoff, a personal crisis, or a changing professional environment. Other times, we simply look around at our circumstances and realize we want something different.

Regardless of how you got to the point where you are considering using this workbook, I encourage you to embrace the fact that you are at a point where you're <u>ready </u>to expand your potential.

Consider that each person you lead is influenced in ways that, in turn, influence whomever they lead. Case in point: the three leadership mentors described earlier are actually impacting YOU at this very moment as a result of their influence on me…quite a powerful ripple effect! Think about it.

So, I recommend you find a comfortable chair, grab a good cup of your favorite warm beverage, and take the time to *Think About It* – the 'it' being your own personal leadership style.

Have fun with this workbook. Approach each session with an open mind and clear head, hi-light those ideas that impact you, dog-ear the pages that most resonate in your heart, and write all over it as the messages, quotes, and coaching exercises trigger insights for you. Refer to it often, re-read it as you face new leadership challenges.

Thank you for the opportunity and privilege to be a part of the personal journey upon which you have embarked.

Mike Malinchok

Some thoughts about *Think About It*.......

"A successful combination of solid coaching strategies, insightful personal observations, and very practical hands-on exercises make *Think About It* an easy-to-use tool for anyone seeking to take their professional game, and life, to the next level."

Bruce D Schneider Ph.D., Author, Energy Leadership

"*Think About It* is a long overdue and essential tool to take a manager's game to the next level. Mike concisely identifies the key areas of differentiation that need to be mastered in order to be a more effective contributor both in and outside of work. After knowing and experiencing Mike for over a decade, I've come to appreciate his sound theory and practical application tips and techniques. His personal insight into situations helps crystalize the concepts into tangible, bite-sized nuggets, suitable for consumption by anyone. It's refreshing to see a real treasure of business acumen stand apart and rise to the top in a sea of management coaching guidebooks in a saturated marketplace. If you're looking for tried and true techniques that will effect real change, I strongly encourage you to turn the page. And if you're already at the top of your organization, it's never too late to have a good self-coaching guidebook at your side. The best always know that they need to continually adapt to new challenges. Good reading and growing!"

Brad Langley, President & CEO

"As my executive coach, Mike helped me prepare for one of the most significant, game-changing interviews of my career. His patience and persistence in having me find the answer to the ultimate questions of "Who am I?" and "What do I do?" were critical pieces of my preparation. This book takes you on a similar journey and Mike does what many others can't do, the book is almost as good as sitting with Mike in person. I applaud his efforts in being able to methodically help you discover your true talents and style so that you can articulate those strengths in key conversations with family, staff and stakeholders."

Donna Peterson, President & CEO

"Successful leadership is the result of a diligent, consistent effort that transforms a personal vision to reality. *Think About It!* suggests that with introspection and discipline, anyone can change their world for the better. Mike has compiled a guide book to help you get focused and serious about personal improvement, and most importantly, he coaches you out of your comfort zone and on the road to meaningful change. It's practical is its approach, effective in its ability to get to the essence of life's obstacles, and positive in its view that everything is possible. Bravo -- this one has something for the leader in all of us!"

John Pino - Chairman, CEO and Founder

"Finally! A handbook that breaks down coaching into categories and checklists, complete with useable templates. If you have been putting off coaching, Mike Malinchok provides you with a head start in this wonderful book. Most books are about concept, but his is different as it focuses on actions that you can take NOW! I plan to recommend this book to my colleagues, family and friends. Thank you, Mike, for your excellent book! "

Debi Scholar, President

"*Think About It is* setup for personal action and change. Mike reveals four key areas of self that we must 'think about'. Once he has your attention he encourages you to take action through a series of exercises designed to help make you accountable. It is a great self-coaching investment constructed by a great coach."

Jack Kelly, Vice President

"This workbook is vital for anyone who is searching for the right resources that will enable a significant forward leap in personal satisfaction, professional advancement and overall life success. Mike Malinchok is a seasoned professional who has journeyed through his life and career capturing thoughtful impressions of the people and experiences that triggered opportunities for growth and transformation. In this workbook, he opens his world and shares these with you and guides you to maximize the earning and growth possibilities of each one. Having worked with Mike as my coach for several years, I challenge you to take full advantage of this valuable tool – I promise you will be pleased with the results."

Linda J. McNairy, Vice President

"*Think About It* provides you with the tools needed to identify your leadership style in a very creative way. The practical techniques outlined in this book empower you to take control of and manage life's decisions whether they be career or personal. You take the initiative in creating your own personal leadership style, helping you reach your best performance. Using the personal stories and relevant self-directed exercises, this workbook helps you achieve, embrace and maximize your own leadership style. While the book is geared to mid-level managers, it will benefit anyone looking to achieve success in work and life."

Sharon Tolliver, Senior Director

"Amazing value: where else can you get the impact of several months and thousands of dollars of world class professional coaching in one concise tool? Michael's wit and wisdom come clearly through in this well written and easy to use workbook. His keen focus on personal accountability and exposing with brutal honesty of where we are versus where we want to be are at the core of his success. Get this workbook, whip out a pen and get ready to dig in – it will be worth every minute you spend. I've been on the receiving end of Michael's support and wisdom for the better part of a decade – we are lucky he's made available his unique perspective and tools for success to the broader audience that is the world. Now take advantage, unlock your personal leadership potential, and LEAD!"

Kari Wendel, Senior Director

"Mike does a fantastic job by setting this book up to be used as a learning tool as well as workbook. The quotes throughout are extremely powerful and the book recommendations are a great little extra. As a leader in the Meetings Industry, I read this as I was going through a career transition and trying to figure out "Who am I" and "What do I do". The overarching message of this book pertains to Personal Leadership. Mike ties in his personal experiences throughout the book which leaves a very powerful impact on the reader; the importance of remembering to be human. This book engaged my mind and took me on a extraordinary self defining journey."

Dana Cronin, SMMC

To the following very special people whose influence on my life and work are deeply woven into the fabric of this workbook:

To KLM, my editor, for polishing my voice and keeping my penchant for ellipses in-check.

To KCM, whose steadfast commitment to the principles she holds dear inspires me to never lose sight of my own.

To SKM, who shows me that passion IS the purpose, and it's no more complicated than that.

To MPM, my original life coach, whose uncompromising standard for professional excellence and formidable classroom presence have inspired my work more deeply than she could have ever known.

And,

To each one of my clients who have placed trust in me to help keep them moving forward on their journey. It is a privilege I never take lightly.

Contents

Overview

This workbook is organized around four foundational pillars of

effective personal leadership:

I. Awareness

II. Discipline

III. Attitude

IV. Influence

Each section commences with a collection of thought
provoking quotes on that particular foundational pillar.

Next, comes 24 coaching 'sessions' that will help you to define and cultivate your own approach to each leadership pillar. Each session includes:

1. Coaching Messages – *Insightful and thought-provoking stories about real life business scenarios that demonstrate the corresponding leadership foundation section theme (Self Awareness, Discipline, Attitude, or Influence) in which the message is found.*

2. A Guided Coaching Journal- *A set of open ended and exploratory questions designed to bring the lesson of the coaching message to life in a very personal way.*

3. Assignments – *Recommended coaching exercises, articles, and books all supporting the points explored in the coaching messages as well as each foundational pillar of leadership.*

Following the last session of the workbook is a comprehensive list of the books which have been recommended for each session in the *Think About It* **Library.**

Following that is the *Think About It* **Tool Kit** which contains the details of the exercises that are also recommended for each session in the book.

About the pictures in this book....

Each image was selected for its power to evoke an emotional connection
to those times, places, and settings in which the reader might be
most likely to engage in introspective thought...the kind that allows
answers to bubble up and solutions to challenges come to light.

AWARENESS

This section centers on raising awareness to self: the understanding of the <u>what you do</u> as well as the how and <u>why you do the things that you do</u> in your professional and personal lives. Foundational to effective leadership, awareness of self is a continual process and not a one-time act. It can be difficult to get started and, if done well, there's a good chance that sometimes you may not like some of things you become aware of about yourself. But, if you persist and cast aside any self-judgment, you will likely find it to be remarkably empowering and energizing.

Awareness
Thought Leadership

There is a voice inside of you that whispers all day long, "I feel that this is right for me, I know that this is wrong.' No teacher, preacher, parent, friend or wise man can decide what is right for you – just listen to the voice that speaks inside.
Shel Silverstein

Hide not your talents, they for use were made. What's a sundial in the shade?
Benjamin Franklin

Don't look for someone in whom to believe. Believe in yourself. The only authentic authority is your own original nature.
Vernon Howard

We are each gifted in a unique and important way. It is our privilege and our adventure to discover our own special light
Mary Dunbar

"What is necessary to change a person is to change his awareness of himself."
Abraham H. Maslow

"Whatever you are, be a good one."
Abraham Lincoln

Awareness
Message 1

Remembering Your Voice

My teenage daughter has embraced the usual angst that comes along with trying to find her place in the world. Like so many of us, she sees clearly the gifts that others seem to have found but struggles to recognize her own.

Recently, as I watched her sing in a local talent contest, something happened. As I listened to her pure, crystal-clear and pitch- perfect performance I was keenly aware that I was witnessing something more profound.

Through her voice in those three and a half minutes of singing 'On My Own' from Les Miserables, the true essence of my daughter became evident as an emerging young woman stepped out from behind the mask of confused teenager. I was not alone in what I felt. The energy in the room shifted (validated by others I spoke with) and the body language of the judges reflected full-on engagement.

It was evident to anyone paying attention that she connected with something inside of herself in a compelling and magnetic way.

The coach in me was moved to be sure she was aware of what happened in those moments which was less about the vocal performance (which, of course, was flawless), and more about her connection to self (which, in my opinion, was profound). My level of pride, which was scraping the ceiling already, shot through the roof when she shared with me that she felt it as well...without me having to bring it to her attention.

My advice to her was this: 'Remember this moment and what you did to make it happen. Don't ever forget it or doubt your ability to manifest it again, and again, and again.'

I work with a lot of mid-career executives who struggle to articulate what they do that brings forth their 'voice'. When clients tell me they don't know what they want or aren't sure of what they do to bring out their voice, I gently but firmly push back on them like this:

You DO know, it's time to remember your voice.

Whether you're a teenager or a mid-career executive trying to figure out what to do with your life...finding and remembering your voice is about connecting your outward actions to your internal core. It's about creating a career or life path that nurtures that voice, as opposed to stifling it or letting it stagnate.

Awareness
Remembering Your Voice
Journal

What drew my attention to this message?

What is going on right now in my world that has caused this topic to resonate with me?

What do I want to make happen in my life (personal or professional) specific to this topic? What would be my desired state in this area of my life if I had no obstacles in front of me?

(be as detailed and specific as possible)

Complete this sentence:

"Once my desired state is manifested (as described above in this area of life), the following will be possible for me:

What is getting in the way of me having this desired state right now in this area of my life?

List as many tangible hurdles that are in the way right now:

i.e. professional credentials, specific equipment, or physical requirements.

List as many intangible hurdles that are in the way right now:

i.e. fears, inner criticism, and other beliefs that limit you

What am I willing to give up in order to pursue the desired state?

i.e. time, comfort, convenience, money

Who do I trust to hold me accountable right now if I share my intentions to take action toward getting what I want in this area of my life?

Name_____

In what way would I want to be held accountable by this person – i.e. check in with me once a week? Once a month? Or 6 months from today? Phone calls, emails, in person visits?

Intention Statement: Fill in the blanks:

As of today (INSERT DATE), I commit to taking the following 3 action steps toward manifesting my desired state in this area of my life:

1.

2.

3.

I will ask (INSERT NAME) to be my accountability coach in this endeavor by opening up to (INSERT DAILY, WEEKLY, MONTHLY) check in (CALLS/EMAILS) until I accomplish these tasks.

Having worked through these journal points, what bubbles up in your mind? *What seems possible that didn't seem possible before? How would you describe your energy level right now? What fears or obstacles continue to seem daunting? What fears or obstacles have diminished a bit?*

Awareness
Remembering Your Voice
Assignment

Below are suggestions specific to this message that are recommended to continue your personal work on this topic. The Exercise sheets (Tool Kit) and List of Books (Library) are located in Section V and VI in the back of the book.

Exercises

The Legacy Letter

Know This

Plug It In

Productize You

Books

A Prayer for Owen Meany

Strengths Finder 2.0

The Dream Manager

Notes

Awareness
Message 2

<u>Be You</u>

At the end of a 90 minute bikram (or 'hot') yoga session I sweated my way through this week, my teacher had the class focus on this succinct meditation. Simple words.....delivering a sagely challenging directive.

I believe two things make this seemingly simple meditation pragmatically challenging..the two words 'be' and 'you':

First, to simply 'be' goes against our obsessive cultural celebration of 'doing'. We reward and promote 'doers'. We eschew the notion of 'being' as something that somehow lacks tangible value and, therefore, is not enough.

Second, the foundational assumption that makes embracing this meditation possible is that we can actually answer the question 'who are you?' in a way other than: 'I am what I do' or 'it depends on who I'm with' or 'do you mean at work or at home?'.

Coaching executive leadership places emphasis on raising a client's level of self-awareness - knowing 'who you are'. Coaches help leaders understand that the way they do <u>one</u> thing, they do ALL things.

The concept is in full alignment with the mediation to 'be you' wherever, whenever and with whomever you find yourself.

In my work I have found that most people aren't as far from knowing the answer as they often think they are. A few well crafted and timed questions create unguarded dialogue that enables clues to emerge. The clues allow me to show a client when he or she is 'BEING YOU'?

1. There's a shift in vocal energy (tone, cadence, pitch) that reveals passion - *'I know exactly what to do'*

2. The roadblocks to goals melt into manageable challenges - *'I can figure this out.'*

3. Outcomes are neutralized - *'it's all good, there's no win or lose'*

4. The inner critic is silenced - *'I can do anything!'*

Robin Sharma, in his book 'The Saint, the Surfer, and the CEO', asserts that we were born with a complete knowledge of ourselves. But in the busy-ness of life (aka 'doing') we get distracted and forget.

He says ' The journey of life is not about *improving* oneself..... rather, it is about *remembering* oneself.'

Something to think about today:

Where, when, and with whom are you experiencing any of the clues listed above?

In other words, when are you most BEING YOU?

Awareness
Be You
Journal

What drew my attention to this message?

What is going on right now in my world that has caused this topic to resonate with me?

What do I want to make happen in my life (personal or professional) specific to this topic? What would be my desired state in this area of my life if I had no obstacles in front of me?

(be as detailed and specific as possible)

Complete this sentence:

"Once my desired state is manifested (as described above in this area of life), the following will be possible for me:

What is getting in the way of me having this desired state right now in this area of my life?

List as many tangible hurdles that are in the way right now:

i.e. professional credentials, specific equipment, or physical requirements.

List as many intangible hurdles that are in the way right now:

i.e. fears, inner criticism, and other beliefs that limit you

What am I willing to give up in order to pursue the desired state?

i.e. time, comfort, convenience, money

Who do I trust to hold me accountable right now if I share my intentions to take action toward getting what I want in this area of my life?

Name_____

In what way would I want to be held accountable by this person – i.e. check in with me once a week? Once a month? Or 6 months from today? Phone calls, emails, in person visits?

Intention Statement: Fill in the blanks:

As of today (INSERT DATE), I commit to taking the following 3 action steps toward manifesting my desired state in this area of my life:

1.

2.

3.

I will ask (INSERT NAME) to be my accountability coach in this endeavor by opening up to (INSERT DAILY, WEEKLY, MONTHLY) check in (CALLS/EMAILS) until I accomplish these tasks.

Having worked through these journal points, what bubbles up in your mind? *What seems possible that didn't seem possible before? How would you describe your energy level right now? What fears or obstacles continue to seem daunting? What fears or obstacles have diminished a bit?*

Awareness
Be You
Assignment

Below are suggestions specific to this message that are recommended to continue your personal work on this topic. The Exercise sheets (Tool Kit) and List of Books (Library) are located in Section V and VI in the back of the book.

Exercises

Know This

Legacy Letter

Choose A Wolf

The Mala & the Mantra

Books

What Should I Do With My Life?

The Good Life

With Purpose

The World According to Garp

Notes

Awareness
Message 3

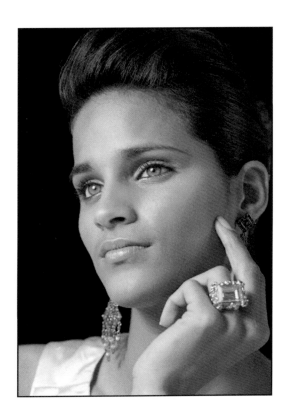

<u>Be Bold</u>

'Freedom lies in being bold.'
Robert Frost

The times call for it, your position requires it, and somewhere deep in your core...you know as well as I do that you have it in you to be bold.

So, just do it - be bold.

It is easy to type but sometimes difficult to put into action.
Why? One word: Fear... the single most powerful emotion that influences the way in which we manage through our days.

Using Webster's dictionary, let's see if we can root out the fears that block our ability to be the bold leaders we know we are.

Follow this sequence:

BOLD: *not hesitating or fearful in the face of actual or possible <u>danger</u>*

DANGER: *the state of being <u>vulnerable</u> to injury or loss*

VULNERABLE: *open to <u>temptation</u>, persuasion, or censure*

TEMPTATION: *to entice or allure to do something regarded as <u>unwise</u> or wrong*

UNWISE: *lacking in good sense or <u>judgment</u>*

JUDGMENT: *the ability to <u>make a decision</u> objectively, authoritatively, and wisely*

When I challenge a client to be bold in facing a leadership situation, there's often a fear-based 'what if' reason that immediately crops up. One way to bust that roadblock is to go through the sequence above and work it through using these questions:

1. What <u>danger</u>, actual or possible exists?

2. To what degree would my boldness create <u>vulnerability</u>?

3. What <u>temptation</u> will become evident in that vulnerability?

4. How might this lead to an <u>unwise outcome or decision</u>?

5. How confident am I in my ability to <u>make a decision wisely</u>?

Bold leadership doesn't change the fact that there will be outcomes as a result of your actions, but, if you are confident in your ability to make wise decisions to manage the outcomes, then I challenge you to identify a fear that you can't work through that would enable your boldness to stand up and take center stage.

One last thought: try not to buy into the myth that a bold leader is someone with a personal style that is one dimensional and different from your own. You can define 'bold' in any way you wish.

So, just do it - be bold.

Awareness
Be Bold
Journal

What drew my attention to this message?

What is going on right now in my world that has caused this topic to resonate with me?

What do I want to make happen in my life (personal or professional) specific to this topic? What would be my desired state in this area of my life if I had no obstacles in front of me?

(be as detailed and specific as possible)

Complete this sentence:

"Once my desired state is manifested (as described above in this area of life), the following will be possible for me:

What is getting in the way of me having this desired state right now in this area of my life?

List as many tangible hurdles that are in the way right now:

i.e. professional credentials, specific equipment, or physical requirements.

List as many intangible hurdles that are in the way right now:

i.e. fears, inner criticism, and other beliefs that limit you

What am I willing to give up in order to pursue the desired state?

i.e. time, comfort, convenience, money

Who do I trust to hold me accountable right now if I share my intentions to take action toward getting what I want in this area of my life?

Name_____

In what way would I want to be held accountable by this person — i.e. check in with me once a week? Once a month? Or 6 months from today? Phone calls, emails, in person visits?

Intention Statement: Fill in the blanks:

As of today (INSERT DATE), I commit to taking the following 3 action steps toward manifesting my desired state in this area of my life:

1.

2.

3.

I will ask (INSERT NAME) to be my accountability coach in this endeavor by opening up to (INSERT DAILY, WEEKLY, MONTHLY) check in (CALLS/EMAILS) until I accomplish these tasks.

Having worked through these journal points, what bubbles up in your mind? *What seems possible that didn't seem possible before? How would you describe your energy level right now? What fears or obstacles continue to seem daunting? What fears or obstacles have diminished a bit?*

Awareness
Be Bold
Assignment

Below are suggestions specific to this message that are recommended to continue your personal work on this topic. The Exercise sheets (Tool Kit) and List of Books (Library) are located in Section V and VI in the back of the book.

Exercises

The Miracle Exercise

Plug It In

Productize You

Books

9 Things a Leader Must Do

Mojo

Well Being

The World According to Garp

Notes

Awareness
Message 4

<u>Lean Into It</u>

It's the most wonderful time of the year..... perhaps.

The end of a calendar year can be a complicated one for many folks. It would be easy to jump on the cultural bandwagon and recite all the reasons why it is a time to be filled with joy, however, I believe there's coaching value in poking at the other side to this time of year.

For some, this is the most energetically draining time of year - tons of work deadlines, closing out sales deals, or wrapping up as many loose ends as possible before taking time away from the office.

Layer this with the emotional impact the holiday season can have and you may find yourself depleted of your personal energy and feeling as though you've hit a wall.

This condition can be disruptive, distracting, and cause distress. In a word, you might look at this as a form of personal suffering that will have direct impact on the way you approach your life and work.

If we were discussing this one-on-one, I'd say things like this to you, inserting personal examples from your past year:

'It's been quite a 12 months....there's been significant things happen to you this year....you have expounded a ton of energy both personally and professionally... you've advanced your career...you've sacrificed much...some goals and aspirations have been met and some have not....some new challenges have been placed on your path.... you've made some strides...you've suffered some terrible losses... you have grown...you are different... you are not the same person you were last year at this time. And, all of that has taken energy.'

Be mindful these coming weeks of your reaction to hitting a wall like this. Rather than dismissing it or driving through it full speed, I encourage you to think about another approach to self-coaching your way through it:

Lean into it.

It might just be exactly where you are supposed to be. It might hold some clues and information that are important for you to understand. It might be serving a more profound purpose in your life.

In this time of reflection, consider some religious perspectives on the concept of suffering:

The Buddhist might say: 'sit with discomfort without trying to fix it, stay present with the pain and let it transform you.'

The Christian might say: "Rom. 5:2-3 - '...more than rejoicing in our hope, we rejoice in our sufferings which produce endurance, character and hope...'

The Sikh might say: 'Suffering is a gift because it connects us to our deepest truth.'

The Rabbi might say: ' You cannot run from suffering, it is an integral part of the process of birth of the self.'

I encourage you to be aware of your energy supply during the coming weeks. If you find yourself experiencing a noticeable drop, try to just allow it and trust that you're not always in this state - this past year gives you enough evidence to show you that it is a temporary state.

If you find your thoughts leaning to either extreme of denying it or embracing it as permanent, try using one of the following phrases to end any thoughts or sentences that start with something like this: "I am completely drained and disconnected...":

....today.

....right now.

....at this moment.

....during this time of year.

Lean into it for a while, see what it brings.

Awareness
Lean Into It
Journal

What drew my attention to this message?

What is going on right now in my world that has caused this topic to resonate with me?

What do I want to make happen in my life (personal or professional) specific to this topic? What would be my desired state in this area of my life if I had no obstacles in front of me?

(be as detailed and specific as possible)

Complete this sentence:

"Once my desired state is manifested (as described above in this area of life), the following will be possible for me:

What is getting in the way of me having this desired state right now in this area of my life?

<u>List as many tangible hurdles that are in the way right now:</u>

i.e. professional credentials, specific equipment, or physical requirements.

<u>List as many intangible hurdles that are in the way right now:</u>

i.e. fears, inner criticism, and other beliefs that limit you

What am I willing to give up in order to pursue the desired state?

i.e. time, comfort, convenience, money

Who do I trust to hold me accountable right now if I share my intentions to take action toward getting what I want in this area of my life?

Name_____

In what way would I want to be held accountable by this person – i.e. check in with me once a week? Once a month? Or 6 months from today? Phone calls, emails, in person visits?

Intention Statement: Fill in the blanks:

As of today (INSERT DATE), I commit to taking the following 3 action steps toward manifesting my desired state in this area of my life:

1.

2.

3.

I will ask (INSERT NAME) to be my accountability coach in this endeavor by opening up to (INSERT DAILY, WEEKLY, MONTHLY) check in (CALLS/EMAILS) until I accomplish these tasks.

Having worked through these journal points, what bubbles up in your mind? *What seems possible that didn't seem possible before? How would you describe your energy level right now? What fears or obstacles continue to seem daunting? What fears or obstacles have diminished a bit?*

Awareness
Lean Into It
Assignment

Below are suggestions specific to this message that are recommended to continue your personal work on this topic. The Exercise sheets (Tool Kit) and List of Books (Library) are located in Section V and VI in the back of the book.

Exercises

The Wheel of Life

G.A.I.L Sheet

Books

The Places that Scare You

Uncomfortable with Uncertainty

The Simple Feeling of Being

Prayer, Faith, and Healing

Notes

Awareness
Message 5

<u>The Books that Find You</u>

This week was a mixed bag of emotions in my family life. My oldest (son) has gone off to college and my youngest (daughter) joins her older sister as a fellow high school student.

My job description as father is undergoing a 're-write' as this time of transition opens up a new set of conditions with different requirements, deliverables, and timelines.

Times of transition tend to bring about anxiety, stress, and a lack of clarity that can be very disconcerting.

For me, times of transition always lead me to books...for insight, ideas, validation, and even for a bit of escape.

My experience has been that the most impactful and important books I have read have been the ones that somehow FOUND ME, not the other way around.

They have not been the NY Times bestsellers, nor the ones by well known authors....but rather the obscure ones that somehow found their way onto my radar screen.

They are the ones about which I can immediately recall where I was when they found me, what situation I was facing, and one or two key takeaways that I incorporated into my life.

This week, I reached for two such books on my shelf that found me over 15 years ago when I was trying to formulate my strategy on the kind of father I would be to my young children.

Once again, these books worked their magic. This time, though, in a slightly fresh way that reconnected me with the broader, deeper sense of purpose I have about my role as father that the emotion-filled milestones were clouding.

They helped to restore clarity.

What powerful, thought-provoking books have found you?

Where were you when they found you?

How did they impact you?

Perhaps today, one or both of the two books that found me were intended to be on your radar screen:

Letters to My Son

by Kent Nerburn

Strong Fathers, Strong Daughters

by Meg Meeker, MD

Awareness
The Books that Find You
Journal

What drew my attention to this message?

What is going on right now in my world that has caused this topic to resonate with me?

What do I want to make happen in my life (personal or professional) specific to this topic? What would be my desired state in this area of my life if I had no obstacles in front of me?

(be as detailed and specific as possible)

Complete this sentence:

"Once my desired state is manifested (as described above in this area of life), the following will be possible for me:

What is getting in the way of me having this desired state right now in this area of my life?

List as many tangible hurdles that are in the way right now:

i.e. professional credentials, specific equipment, or physical requirements.

List as many intangible hurdles that are in the way right now:

i.e. fears, inner criticism, and other beliefs that limit you

What am I willing to give up in order to pursue the desired state?

i.e. time, comfort, convenience, money

Who do I trust to hold me accountable right now if I share my intentions to take action toward getting what I want in this area of my life?

Name_____

In what way would I want to be held accountable by this person – i.e. check in with me once a week? Once a month? Or 6 months from today? Phone calls, emails, in person visits?

Intention Statement: Fill in the blanks:

As of today (INSERT DATE), I commit to taking the following 3 action steps toward manifesting my desired state in this area of my life:

1.

2.

3.

I will ask (INSERT NAME) to be my accountability coach in this endeavor by opening up to (INSERT DAILY, WEEKLY, MONTHLY) check in (CALLS/EMAILS) until I accomplish these tasks.

Having worked through these journal points, what bubbles up in your mind? *What seems possible that didn't seem possible before? How would you describe your energy level right now? What fears or obstacles continue to seem daunting? What fears or obstacles have diminished a bit?*

Awareness
The Books that Find You
Assignment

Below are suggestions specific to this message that are recommended to continue your personal work on this topic. The Exercise sheets (Tool Kit) and List of Books (Library) are located in Section V and VI in the back of the book.

Exercises

Books for Life

Books

A Prayer for Own Meany

Necessary Endings

Well Being

Notes

Awareness
Message 6

<u>Head Shot or Candid</u>

"To sit for one's portrait is like being present at one's creation"
Alexander Smith

It is common knowledge that a picture says more than 1,000 words - but does it always tell the truth?

I would say that every photograph tells 'a' truth. It can tell the subject's version of a truth, the photographer's interpretation

of a truth, or in the case of a candid photo...it can reveal
a truth that is neither created nor embellished.

Let's look at two types of photographs through the lens of truth say-er:

Professional photos (Head Shots) - we've all likely had them taken at some time in our careers. They reveal what we want to project. We control the lighting, the backdrop, the wardrobe, the facial expression and tilt of the head. We have the ability to project 'a' truth about ourselves that we choose to ... i.e. I'm serious, I'm trustworthy, I'm successful, I'm sincere. When I'm working with clients, I listen for the 'head shot moments' when I hear things that sound like they come from a sales brochure or when I sense that the words are saying one thing while the energy and spirit in the voice are saying something else. There are times when leading with a headshot is best and there are times when leading with a headshot can be limiting or distracting.

Candids - These types of photos that tell truths that are engaging, compelling, and revealing. Some make us cringe with humility and others warm our heart when something deep inside of us has been captured on film: things like pure joy, absolute passion, or unbridled pride. When I'm in conversations with clients, I liken candid photos to those unguarded moments when a deep 'truth' is somehow slipped into the conversation - either by what is being said or what is not being said. Those are the moments I listen for, bring to my client's attention, and explore (or, as I like to say, 'poke at'.) These 'candid truths' prompt me to say 'tell me more about that' because they reveal depth and texture that is compelling. Candids are like windows into THE truth about a person which ultimately holds the answers to busting through the roadblocks.

I encourage you to get to know what your own 'candids'
look like and what they reveal about you.

Here's a few questions to help you find the candids (be
completely unfiltered and honest as you answer each):

*The last time you hit a successful achievement, what's
the very first thing you did or thought of?*

*The last time you were completely frustrated or angry with
someone, what's the very first thing you did or thought of?*

*This morning, as you looked over your plans for the day, which item on your agenda
brought you the most sense of joy? Which brought you the most sense of dread?*

*If your boss walked in today and gave you carte blanche to 'fix'
any problem you are having in your current situation (open
budget, no restraints...just fix it)...what would you do?*

*If you could be doing anything for a living other than what you are
currently doing, what would it be? Why are you not doing that today?*

This week, try to identify three times when you have
led with the 'Head Shot' version of you and three times
when you've shared the 'Candids' version of you.

Awareness
Head Shot or Candid
Journal

What drew my attention to this message?

What is going on right now in my world that has caused this topic to resonate with me?

What do I want to make happen in my life (personal or professional) specific to this topic? What would be my desired state in this area of my life if I had no obstacles in front of me?

(be as detailed and specific as possible)

Complete this sentence:

"Once my desired state is manifested (as described above in this area of life), the following will be possible for me:

What is getting in the way of me having this desired state right now in this area of my life?

List as many tangible hurdles that are in the way right now:

i.e. professional credentials, specific equipment, or physical requirements.

List as many intangible hurdles that are in the way right now:

i.e. fears, inner criticism, and other beliefs that limit you

What am I willing to give up in order to pursue the desired state?

i.e. time, comfort, convenience, money

Who do I trust to hold me accountable right now if I share my intentions to take action toward getting what I want in this area of my life?

Name_____

In what way would I want to be held accountable by this person – i.e. check in with me once a week? Once a month? Or 6 months from today? Phone calls, emails, in person visits?

Intention Statement: Fill in the blanks:

As of today (INSERT DATE), I commit to taking the following 3 action steps toward manifesting my desired state in this area of my life:

1.

2.

3.

I will ask (INSERT NAME) to be my accountability coach in this endeavor by opening up to (INSERT DAILY, WEEKLY, MONTHLY) check in (CALLS/EMAILS) until I accomplish these tasks.

Having worked through these journal points, what bubbles up in your mind? *What seems possible that didn't seem possible before? How would you describe your energy level right now? What fears or obstacles continue to seem daunting? What fears or obstacles have diminished a bit?*

Awareness
Head Shot or Candid
Assignment

Below are suggestions specific to this message that are recommended to continue your personal work on this topic. The Exercise sheets (Tool Kit) and List of Books (Library) are located in Section V and VI in the back of the book.

<u>Exercises</u>

Productize You

Plug It In

<u>Books</u>

With Purpose

The Power of Self Coaching

Strengths Finder 2.0

Notes

_____

_____

_____

_____

_____

_____

_____

_____

_____

_____

_____

_____

_____

_____

_____

_____

_____

_____

_____

_____

_____

_____

_____

_____

_____

_____

Leadership Foundation II

DISCIPLINE

This section is focused around the principles of managing self, some might call 'self-discipline'. With a realistic understanding of self from Section I, we move now into the art of working with what you have and are. Being an effective leader is not about modeling someone else, it's about being the best 'you' possible. It's about managing your assets and liabilities in a way that yields the best results possible.

Discipline
Thought Leadership

Everyone has talent. What is rare is the courage to follow the talent to the dark place where it leads.
Erica Yong

When you are looking in the mirror, you are looking at the problem. But, remember, you are also looking at the solution.
Anonymous

Your time is limited, so don't waste it living someone else's life. Don't be trapped by dogma – which is living with the results of other people's thinking. Don't let the noise of others' opinions drown out your own inner voice. And most important, have the courage to follow your heart and intuition.
Steve Jobs

"Leaders aren't born, they are made. And they are made just like anything else, through hard work. And that's the price we'll have to pay to achieve that goal, or any goal."
Vince Lombardi

"The ultimate measure of a man is not where he stands in moments of comfort, but where he stands at times of challenge and controversy."
Martin Luther King, Jr.

"Nothing so conclusively proves a man's ability to lead others as what he does from day to day to lead himself."
Thomas J. Watson

"Confront your inadequacies and push your personal boundaries: It's the surest way to grow, improve and expand the scope of your influence."
John Maxwell

"Personal leadership is not a singular experience. It is, rather, the ongoing process of keeping your vision and values before you and aligning your life to be congruent with those most important things."
Stephen Covey

Discipline
Message 1

<u>Choose a Wolf</u>

If you're not familiar with the Cherokee Legend of Two Wolves, take a few moments to read the brief fable located in the back of this book (Number 4 in the Self Coaching Tool Box section) .

If you are already familiar with it , then you know the premise of the story that speaks to our personal power of choosing which 'wolf' to feed help manifest the things we most want in our lives.

The decision of which wolf to feed is quickly followed by establishing a strategy around exactly WHAT to feed that chosen wolf to insure its health.

Good books are one type of 'food' that can
nourish the 'wolves' within our minds.

Right now is the perfect time to recommit to areas of growth and
personal development that you intuitively KNOW are needed, but
perhaps you've lacked the push to actually do something about it.

Take a few minutes right now, decide which
'wolf' you are going to feed this fall.

Don't stop there...go further... decide exactly HOW will you
feed that 'wolf'... (i.e. books, lectures, personal coaching).

What daily tasks will you incorporate into your life
that will nourish that 'wolf' (i.e. meditation, reading a
goals sheet, absorbing a motivational mantra)?

What kinds of people will you actively seek to spend MORE time with
that serve as nourishment for that 'wolf' (i.e. mentors, coaches, teachers)?

Which type of person will you pro-actively spend LESS time
with so as to minimize any unnecessary diversion from feeding
your chosen 'wolf'? (identify by name, if necessary)

And, finally, decide today to embrace this Indian legend and its gift of
raising your self-awareness to one of the most powerful self-leadership tools
available to you RIGHT NOW....your power to choose *which wolf will win*.

Discipline
Choose a Wolf
Journal

What drew my attention to this message?

What is going on right now in my world that has caused this topic to resonate with me?

What do I want to make happen in my life (personal or professional) specific to this topic? What would be my desired state in this area of my life if I had no obstacles in front of me?

(be as detailed and specific as possible)

Complete this sentence:

"Once my desired state is manifested (as described above in this area of life), the following will be possible for me:

What is getting in the way of me having this desired state right now in this area of my life?

List as many tangible hurdles that are in the way right now:

i.e. professional credentials, specific equipment, or physical requirements.

List as many intangible hurdles that are in the way right now:

i.e. fears, inner criticism, and other beliefs that limit you

What am I willing to give up in order to pursue the desired state?

i.e. time, comfort, convenience, money

Who do I trust to hold me accountable right now if I share my intentions to take action toward getting what I want in this area of my life?

Name_____

In what way would I want to be held accountable by this person – i.e. check in with me once a week? Once a month? Or 6 months from today? Phone calls, emails, in person visits?

Intention Statement: Fill in the blanks:

As of today (INSERT DATE), I commit to taking the following 3 action steps toward manifesting my desired state in this area of my life:

1.

2.

3.

I will ask (INSERT NAME) to be my accountability coach in this endeavor by opening up to (INSERT DAILY, WEEKLY, MONTHLY) check in (CALLS/EMAILS) until I accomplish these tasks.

Having worked through these journal points, what bubbles up in your mind? *What seems possible that didn't seem possible before? How would you describe your energy level right now? What fears or obstacles continue to seem daunting? What fears or obstacles have diminished a bit?*

Discipline
Choose a Wolf
Assignment

Below are suggestions specific to this message that are recommended to continue your personal work on this topic. The Exercise sheets (Tool Kit) and List of Books (Library) are located in Section V and VI in the back of the book.

<u>Exercises</u>

Choose a Wolf

G.A.I.L. Sheet

The Miracle Exercise

Know This

<u>Books</u>

The Sedona Method

Well Being

The Power of Self Coaching

Notes

_____
_____
_____
_____
_____
_____
_____
_____
_____
_____
_____
_____
_____
_____
_____
_____
_____
_____
_____
_____
_____
_____
_____
_____
_____
_____
_____

Discipline
Message 2

<u>The Space in Between</u>

"I know that something has to change.

BUT, the devil I know...."

Most times, we are aware that we need to change,

but we are blocked by fear:

The fear that if we give up what we have, do, or know, the alternative could be worse, more difficult, or harmful. And so, we decide that the "devil" we know might not be so bad to live with until we have something known, proven, and low-risk to replace it with. This can often result in long-term inertia as we grow more and more fearful of that "devil" we haven't met yet.

One way to break that cycle is to allow yourself to just simply cease the existing behavior you want to change and give yourself some breathing room. Don't think about replacing or filling in the space just yet, relax and enjoy the task of making space.

(Like that cathartic feeling of cleaning out the basement, garage, or attic)

Pema Chodron, in her book The Places that Scare you, refers to this place as "the *in between* state where the warrior spends a lot of time growing up". It is the place that she says, 'by not knowing, not hoping to know, and not acting like we know what's happening

we access our inner strength".

It's a place where our <u>skills are called into action</u>, our <u>resolve is put to the test</u>, and <u>our faith becomes more than a theory</u>.

Next time you find yourself even thinking "The devil I know.."

......try one of these endings:

1. Could be 10 times worse than the devil I haven't met yet...

2. Is choking the life out of me .....

3. Has tricked me into thinking this is the best it will ever be...

These might just make the 'in between' spaces less intimidating.

Discipline
The Space in Between
Journal

What drew my attention to this message?

What is going on right now in my world that has caused this topic to resonate with me?

What do I want to make happen in my life (personal or professional) specific to this topic? What would be my desired state in this area of my life if I had no obstacles in front of me?

(be as detailed and specific as possible)

Complete this sentence:

"Once my desired state is manifested (as described above in this area of life), the following will be possible for me:

What is getting in the way of me having this desired state right now in this area of my life?

List as many tangible hurdles that are in the way right now:

i.e. professional credentials, specific equipment, or physical requirements.

List as many intangible hurdles that are in the way right now:

i.e. fears, inner criticism, and other beliefs that limit you

What am I willing to give up in order to pursue the desired state?

i.e. time, comfort, convenience, money

Who do I trust to hold me accountable right now if I share my intentions to take action toward getting what I want in this area of my life?

Name_____

In what way would I want to be held accountable by this person — i.e. check in with me once a week? Once a month? Or 6 months from today? Phone calls, emails, in person visits?

Intention Statement: Fill in the blanks:

As of today (INSERT DATE), I commit to taking the following 3 action steps toward manifesting my desired state in this area of my life:

1.

2.

3.

I will ask (INSERT NAME) to be my accountability coach in this endeavor by opening up to (INSERT DAILY, WEEKLY, MONTHLY) check in (CALLS/EMAILS) until I accomplish these tasks.

Having worked through these journal points, what bubbles up in your mind? *What seems possible that didn't seem possible before? How would you describe your energy level right now? What fears or obstacles continue to seem daunting? What fears or obstacles have diminished a bit?*

Discipline
The Space in Between
Assignment

Below are suggestions specific to this message that are recommended to continue your personal work on this topic. The Exercise sheets (Tool Kit) and List of Books (Library) are located in Section V and VI in the back of the book.

Exercises

The Peasant and Zemyne

Change versus Transformation

Books

The Places that Scare You

Comfortable with Uncertainty

What Should I Do With My Life?

Notes

Discipline
Message 3

<u>Nurture the Spark</u>

I am always humbled by the generous feedback The Second Cup readers share with me. The responses I receive infuse me with a sense of purpose and gratitude that is invigorating.

While there is a consistent level of feedback (number of responses), there is a fair amount of inconsistency around which readers generate that feedback. It seems that each edition resonates differently with different segments of the readership base.

In terms of motivation and commitment to change, this validates to me the existence of two important ingredients that influence successful self-coaching toward a new goal:

1. CONTENT

The message must be clear, accurate, and concise.

2. TIMING

That serendipitous condition that gives you pause to say

"I really needed to hear that today".

Content and Timing.....put the two together and a spark is created. Your attention is gained and there is the <u>potential</u> to ignite a 'fire in the belly'.

Unfortunately, too many stop at the spark. They miss the most critical component that is COMPLETELY within their control:

3. NURTURE

Sparks need fuel to keep them from quickly going out.

Recognizing the spark is worthless unless you actually do something with it! Accept that some force outside of self brought forth the magical potential of the right message at the right time.

Don't let that opportunity for relevant personal growth and change slip through your hands.

Discipline
Nurture the Spark
Journal

What drew my attention to this message?

What is going on right now in my world that has caused this topic to resonate with me?

What do I want to make happen in my life (personal or professional) specific to this topic? What would be my desired state in this area of my life if I had no obstacles in front of me?

(be as detailed and specific as possible)

Complete this sentence:

"Once my desired state is manifested (as described above in this area of life), the following will be possible for me:

What is getting in the way of me having this desired state right now in this area of my life?

List as many tangible hurdles that are in the way right now:

i.e. professional credentials, specific equipment, or physical requirements.

List as many intangible hurdles that are in the way right now:

i.e. fears, inner criticism, and other beliefs that limit you

What am I willing to give up in order to pursue the desired state?

i.e. time, comfort, convenience, money

Who do I trust to hold me accountable right now if I share my intentions to take action toward getting what I want in this area of my life?

Name_____

In what way would I want to be held accountable by this person – i.e. check in with me once a week? Once a month? Or 6 months from today? Phone calls, emails, in person visits?

Intention Statement: Fill in the blanks:

As of today (INSERT DATE), I commit to taking the following 3 action steps toward manifesting my desired state in this area of my life:

1.

2.

3.

I will ask (INSERT NAME) to be my accountability coach in this endeavor by opening up to (INSERT DAILY, WEEKLY, MONTHLY) check in (CALLS/EMAILS) until I accomplish these tasks.

Having worked through these journal points, what bubbles up in your mind? *What seems possible that didn't seem possible before? How would you describe your energy level right now? What fears or obstacles continue to seem daunting? What fears or obstacles have diminished a bit?*

Discipline
Nurture the Spark
Assignment

Below are suggestions specific to this message that are recommended to continue your personal work on this topic. The Exercise sheets (Tool Kit) and List of Books (Library) are located in Section V and VI in the back of the book.

<u>Exercises</u>

Know This

Plug It In

<u>Books</u>

Necessary Endings

Outliers

The Dream Manager

The Good Life

Notes

Discipline
Message 4

<u>Own the Suck</u>

Today (January 1) sucks....

When the alarm went off this morning, your waking thought was likely about a commitment to change something starting TODAY....

i.e. your diet, your engagement to fitness, or perhaps your approach to a challenging relationship at home or at work.

You have decided to replace at least one outdated behavioral pattern with a new one in order to create a new paradigm in your life. Congratulations for taking that on!

As exciting and positive as the change results will be, there is no sugar-coating the fact that changing habits (even bad ones) causes pain. And, until recently, you've been avoiding the pain of change because, well.....pain sucks.

And we don't like what sucks.

Rather than dismiss it or try to 'magically' rise above it with motivational New Year's quotes, I propose you actually chase it down, grab hold of it, and make love to it if need be.

In other words:

OWN THE SUCK.

Three ways to do that:

1. <u>Understand it</u> for what it is:

If you're feeling the 'suck' today, it means that you've hit a nerve that will take you forward. The root cause of the 'suck' is where the solution to your desired goal lies – stay there!

2. <u>Articulate it</u> so as to reduce its mystique:

find the words to express exactly what 'sucks'. Giving it shape and form reduces its power....it puts the control back into your hands.

3. <u>Offset it</u> for balance:

neutralize the draining impact on you with some type of energizing reward. Honor the need to acknowledge and reward your agreement to own the suck. Don't be a martyr....reward yourself as often as you need to.

So, this week, as you approach the new year goals you've set for yourself................take a deep breath and repeat this mantra three times:

OWN THE SUCK.

Discipline
Own the Suck
Journal

What drew my attention to this message?

What is going on right now in my world that has caused this topic to resonate with me?

What do I want to make happen in my life (personal or professional) specific to this topic? What would be my desired state in this area of my life if I had no obstacles in front of me?

(be as detailed and specific as possible)

Complete this sentence:

"Once my desired state is manifested (as described above in this area of life), the following will be possible for me:

What is getting in the way of me having this desired state right now in this area of my life?

List as many tangible hurdles that are in the way right now:

i.e. professional credentials, specific equipment, or physical requirements.

List as many intangible hurdles that are in the way right now:

i.e. fears, inner criticism, and other beliefs that limit you

What am I willing to give up in order to pursue the desired state?

i.e. time, comfort, convenience, money

Who do I trust to hold me accountable right now if I share my intentions to take action toward getting what I want in this area of my life?

Name_____

In what way would I want to be held accountable by this person – i.e. check in with me once a week? Once a month? Or 6 months from today? Phone calls, emails, in person visits?

Intention Statement: Fill in the blanks:

As of today (INSERT DATE), I commit to taking the following 3 action steps toward manifesting my desired state in this area of my life:

1.

2.

3.

I will ask (INSERT NAME) to be my accountability coach in this endeavor by opening up to (INSERT DAILY, WEEKLY, MONTHLY) check in (CALLS/EMAILS) until I accomplish these tasks.

Having worked through these journal points, what bubbles up in your mind? *What seems possible that didn't seem possible before? How would you describe your energy level right now? What fears or obstacles continue to seem daunting? What fears or obstacles have diminished a bit?*

Discipline
Own the Suck
Assignment

Below are suggestions specific to this message that are recommended to continue your personal work on this topic. The Exercise sheets (Tool Kit) and List of Books (Library) are located in Section V and VI in the back of the book.

Exercises

Choose a Wolf

Change versus Transformation

Books

Truman

The Greatest Generation

Personal History

John Adams

Prayer, Faith, and Healing

Notes

Discipline
Message 5

<u>Burn the Dress</u>

In the previous message in this workbook I shared with you the mantra 'Own The Suck' as a way to grab hold of the pain of change and control it versus it controlling you.

The timing of that message intentionally coincided with the after-glow of the holiday season when your engagement to your motivational drivers was most likely very fresh.

Perhaps now, when you are reading this message, you are several weeks down the road and there's a good likelihood that the engagement to your motivation may be getting a bit stale. As we get further away from the holidays, I encourage you to be mindful of just how powerful old habits and familiar thought patterns are.

Often times, those old habits can subtly creep back into our minds in incremental ways that don't even hit our radar screen on a daily basis. If we're not diligent and mindful of them, they can very rapidly take control and derail us from achieving our goals.

You've no doubt heard the phrase *'think outside the box'*. Whether you are facing a set of near year resolutions or making the transition to a new leadership role in your organization, change requires thinking that is different from the what *was* (the box). And while this is an important first step - it's not the full solution.

Not only must you THINK outside the box, but you have to actually DESTROY the box. You have to make it go away, no longer a viable or even possible option.

Otherwise, it's waiting............lurking.........
seductively 'calling out' to you to return.

To best illustrate this point, I encourage you to read 'The Peasant & Zemyne' in the Tool Box section in the back of this book.

Once you do, you'll see why this message is entitled what it is:

Burn the Dress!

Discipline
Burn the Dress
Journal

What drew my attention to this message?

What is going on right now in my world that has caused this topic to resonate with me?

What do I want to make happen in my life (personal or professional) specific to this topic? What would be my desired state in this area of my life if I had no obstacles in front of me?

(be as detailed and specific as possible)

Complete this sentence:

"Once my desired state is manifested (as described above in this area of life), the following will be possible for me:

What is getting in the way of me having this desired state right now in this area of my life?

List as many tangible hurdles that are in the way right now:

i.e. professional credentials, specific equipment, or physical requirements.

List as many intangible hurdles that are in the way right now:

i.e. fears, inner criticism, and other beliefs that limit you

What am I willing to give up in order to pursue the desired state?

i.e. time, comfort, convenience, money

Who do I trust to hold me accountable right now if I share my intentions to take action toward getting what I want in this area of my life?

Name_____

In what way would I want to be held accountable by this person – i.e. check in with me once a week? Once a month? Or 6 months from today? Phone calls, emails, in person visits?

Intention Statement: Fill in the blanks:

As of today (INSERT DATE), I commit to taking the following 3 action steps toward manifesting my desired state in this area of my life:

1.

2.

3.

I will ask (INSERT NAME) to be my accountability coach in this endeavor by opening up to (INSERT DAILY, WEEKLY, MONTHLY) check in (CALLS/EMAILS) until I accomplish these tasks.

Having worked through these journal points, what bubbles up in your mind? *What seems possible that didn't seem possible before? How would you describe your energy level right now? What fears or obstacles continue to seem daunting? What fears or obstacles have diminished a bit?*

Discipline
Burn the Dress
Assignment

Below are suggestions specific to this message that are recommended to continue your personal work on this topic. The Exercise sheets (Tool Kit) and List of Books (Library) are located in Section V and VI in the back of the book.

<u>Exercises</u>

The Peasant and Zemyne

G.A.I.L. Sheet

<u>Books</u>

Necessary Endings

Mojo

Outliers

The World According to Garp

Notes

Discipline
Message 6

<u>Stop Being That</u>

"I'm my own worst enemy..."

The above quote could likely be attributed to each of us at some point in our professional or personal lives. It is seductively simple to allow this into our thinking and it can be the single most impactful negative force in limiting our quest for personal success and contentment.   So, here's a rather obvious coaching suggestion for you:

<u>Stop being that.</u>

A blunt, and rather dismissive suggestion I know, however I

would challenge anyone to come up with any kind of substantive argument for the opposite position - 'Keep being that'.

So, if you agree with me, instead of being your own worst enemy, try this role: Be your own 'best coach'.   Instead of spending your energy on feeding into your limitations, become the advocate for all the strengths, talents, and sources of power that you are uniquely and specifically in possession of.

To help you get started in this new role, here are five professional coaching principles that I spend a few moments focusing on prior to every client session I conduct. Imagine how these principles might help you in your approach to this new role with your own client (yourself) next time he/she is facing a challenge and being his/her own worst enemy:

1. <u>See your client as much more than the current situation.</u>

Actively look for the greatness within your client - find
it, name it, and refer to it often in your sessions.

2. <u>Be gentle with your client.</u> Demonstrate compassion and
empathy for the life journey your client is on. Try to understand
the ways in which it has brought them to this place that
calls for assistance from you, their personal coach.

3. <u>Be fearless in confronting your client's limiting beliefs,</u>
<u>assumptions, interpretations and inner critical voice.</u>

Relentlessly insist on facts to support any thought patterns
your client expresses which keep the session trapped
in the problem versus finding the solution.

4. <u>Trust your intuition.</u> You are capable of seeing and hearing much
more than what is being said. Listen for what is not being said.

5. <u>Connect to your Higher Source.</u> Center your thoughts and
energy to serve your client with the very best you have to offer.

"Most of the shadows of this life are caused by our standing in our own sunshine."
Ralph Waldo Emerson

Discipline
Stop Being That
Journal

What drew my attention to this message?

What is going on right now in my world that has caused this topic to resonate with me?

What do I want to make happen in my life (personal or professional) specific to this topic? What would be my desired state in this area of my life if I had no obstacles in front of me?

(be as detailed and specific as possible)

Complete this sentence:

"Once my desired state is manifested (as described above in this area of life), the following will be possible for me:

What is getting in the way of me having this desired state right now in this area of my life?

List as many tangible hurdles that are in the way right now:

i.e. professional credentials, specific equipment, or physical requirements.

List as many intangible hurdles that are in the way right now:

i.e. fears, inner criticism, and other beliefs that limit you

What am I willing to give up in order to pursue the desired state?

i.e. time, comfort, convenience, money

Who do I trust to hold me accountable right now if I share my intentions to take action toward getting what I want in this area of my life?

Name_____

In what way would I want to be held accountable by this person – i.e. check in with me once a week? Once a month? Or 6 months from today? Phone calls, emails, in person visits?

Intention Statement: Fill in the blanks:

As of today (INSERT DATE), I commit to taking the following 3 action steps toward manifesting my desired state in this area of my life:

1.

2.

3.

I will ask (INSERT NAME) to be my accountability coach in this endeavor by opening up to (INSERT DAILY, WEEKLY, MONTHLY) check in (CALLS/EMAILS) until I accomplish these tasks.

Having worked through these journal points, what bubbles up in your mind? *What seems possible that didn't seem possible before? How would you describe your energy level right now? What fears or obstacles continue to seem daunting? What fears or obstacles have diminished a bit?*

Discipline
Stop Being That
Assignment

Below are suggestions specific to this message that are recommended to continue your personal work on this topic. The Exercise sheets (Tool Kit) and List of Books (Library) are located in Section V and VI in the back of the book.

Exercises

G.A.I.L. Sheet

The Miracle Exercise

Plug It In

Books

The Dream Manager

Truman

Well Being

The Saint, the Surfer, and the CEO

Notes

Leadership Foundation III

ATTITUDE

Is the glass half full or half empty? It's all in your attitude and the attitudes of those for whom you play a leadership role. Attitudes are not static, they change and are influenced by many factors. And, often, we need to recognize that our own attitude needs periodic coaching to retain a leadership edge. This section brings into focus the power of coaching attitudes in order to grow your own effectiveness as a leader.

Attitude
Thought Leadership

A great deal of talent is lost to the world for the want of a little courage.
Sydney Smith

A real leader faces the music, even when he doesn't like the tune.
Anonymous

There are no failures – just experiences and your reactions to them.
Tom Krause

All of us, whether or not we are warriors, have a cubic centimeter of chance that pops out in front of our eyes from time to time. The difference between the average person and a warrior is that the warrior is aware of this and stays alert, deliberately waiting, so that when this cubic centimeter of chance pops out, it is picked up."
Carlos Castaneda

What looks like a loss may be the very event which is subsequently responsible for helping produce the major achievement of your life.
Srully D. Blotnick

Success consists of going from failure to failure without loss of enthusiasm.
Winston Churchill

The ability to summon positive emotions during periods of intense stress lies at the heart of effective leadership.
Jim Loehr

You are the only person who can label what you do a failure. Failure is subjective.
John Maxwell

The artist is nothing without the gift, the gift is nothing without work.
Emile Zola

Attitude
Message 1

<u>The Serenity Formula</u>

'Grant me the serenity to accept the things I cannot change,

the courage to change the things I can, and

the wisdom to know the difference.'

There's a strong chance that you can recite the 'Serenity Prayer' from memory, as it is a timeless classic.

While I embrace the core message and strive for its lofty ideals, there are times when I need a more empowering and personal 'kick in the butt' to get me through the internal roadblocks of a challenging situation.

So, at the risk of being chastised for tinkering with a classic, I am going to see if a few word replacements can shift the energetic tone of this classic to a more action oriented and self-empowering one.

Breaking it down by line:

from *The Serenity Prayer* to <u>*The Serenity Formula*</u>

- Knowing the 'formula' gives you the power and the ingredients to solve your own problem and give yourself that sense of serenity.

from *God grant me* to <u>*within me always*</u> - the self-management tools in this formula are within you, not out 'there' somewhere...they have already been granted.

from *the* to <u>*my*</u>

- these tools are <u>yours</u>, take ownership of them.

from *serenity* to <u>*capacity*</u>

- This part is the toughest one and there is nothing 'serene' about getting yourself to a place of acceptance of this. It often means tapping into reserves of strengths and faith that you sometimes forget you have. It is about remembering that your capacity is often greater than you think.

from *courage* to <u>*ambition*</u>

- courage is a good start, but it is ambition that will drive you to bust through obstacles to achieve results.

from *wisdom* to <u>*instinct*</u>

- Acumen is that 'gut level' talent for discernment which comes from a combination of wisdom, experience, vision, and instinct.

Now, let's put it together:

<u>*The Serenity Formula*</u>

Within me always is

<u>My capacity</u> to accept the things I cannot change

My <u>ambition</u> to change the things I can change

and my <u>instinct</u> to know the difference.

Knowing you have these three powerful self-leadership tools
at your fingertips is certainly a cause for being thankful.
And gratitude is usually the precursor to serenity.

Attitude
The Serenity Formula
Journal

What drew my attention to this message?

What is going on right now in my world that has caused this topic to resonate with me?

What do I want to make happen in my life (personal or professional) specific to this topic? What would be my desired state in this area of my life if I had no obstacles in front of me?

(be as detailed and specific as possible)

Complete this sentence:

"Once my desired state is manifested (as described above in this area of life), the following will be possible for me:

What is getting in the way of me having this desired state right now in this area of my life?

List as many tangible hurdles that are in the way right now:

i.e. professional credentials, specific equipment, or physical requirements.

List as many intangible hurdles that are in the way right now:

i.e. fears, inner criticism, and other beliefs that limit you

What am I willing to give up in order to pursue the desired state?

i.e. time, comfort, convenience, money

Who do I trust to hold me accountable right now if I share my intentions to take action toward getting what I want in this area of my life?

Name_____

In what way would I want to be held accountable by this person – i.e. check in with me once a week? Once a month? Or 6 months from today? Phone calls, emails, in person visits?

Intention Statement: Fill in the blanks:

As of today (INSERT DATE), I commit to taking the following 3 action steps toward manifesting my desired state in this area of my life:

1.

2.

3.

I will ask (INSERT NAME) to be my accountability coach in this endeavor by opening up to (INSERT DAILY, WEEKLY, MONTHLY) check in (CALLS/EMAILS) until I accomplish these tasks.

Having worked through these journal points, what bubbles up in your mind? *What seems possible that didn't seem possible before? How would you describe your energy level right now? What fears or obstacles continue to seem daunting? What fears or obstacles have diminished a bit?*

Attitude
The Serenity Formula
Assignment

Below are suggestions specific to this message that are recommended to continue your personal work on this topic. The Exercise sheets (Tool Kit) and List of Books (Library) are located in Section V and VI in the back of the book.

<u>Exercises</u>

The Miracle Exercise

Plug It In

The Mala & the Mantra

<u>Books</u>

A Prayer for Own Meany

With Purpose

When You Are Engulfed In Flames

Notes

Attitude
Message 2

<u>Put it Back</u>

Ever change your mind about a retail store item you were in the checkout line to purchase?

Or, have you ever been 7 aisles away from where you picked up a grocery item when you decided you were not going to purchase it any longer?

Did you put it back where it belonged, where you found it? Or did you leave it wherever was most convenient for you for someone else to put back?

Last week, I was waiting to checkout at the grocery store as I observed a very important corporate executive brokering a business deal on her cell phone that would solve at least one major world crises right there in front of me. While talking on her phone and surveying her cart, she changed her mind about purchasing 8 out of the 20 items she had gathered.

Rather than put them back where she found them, she not-sodiscreetly crammed them into the soda cooler near the checkout stand. I watched her pretty intently and affixed my gaze on her actions.

We traded eye contact so I know that she knew I was watching her do this.

Had I observed one of my kids doing this, the 'put it back' lecture would have been delivered in full 'annoying *Dad*-voice' with just one acceptable behavioral response to shut me up. *(return the items where they belonged)*

Her actions, in isolation and not knowing her background, lead me to conclude that there are two possible reasons for her behavior:

Either

1. She lacks the APTITUDE to put things back.

It is entirely possible that the woman has never had formal training in 'reverse shopping'. She may never have been taught the skills and techniques involved in putting things back where they were found. In which case, I can't fault her for not performing a function she simply doesn't know how to do.

Or

2. She has an ATTITUDE of arrogance

Given my observations, I can imagine that someone who is so important in her work world yet still required to perform such a tactical function as grocery shopping might likely have been taught that it is ok to draw the line at reverse shopping.

And so, in her world, letting that task fall to someone else is completely acceptable.

If I knew more of her back story, I'm sure I could figure out what was on display that day - was it limited aptitude or an arrogant attitude?

We've all changed our mind in the grocery store and we've all

done some version of what this woman did. In the grand scheme
of things, this might seem trivial - but, take note of yourself
next time you're in the situation - what will you do?

Think about this:

If character is what you do when no one is watching, what
is revealed by what you do when you are being watched
and the impact of your actions visible to others?

Attitude
Put it Back
Journal

What drew my attention to this message?

What is going on right now in my world that has caused this topic to resonate with me?

What do I want to make happen in my life (personal or professional) specific to this topic? What would be my desired state in this area of my life if I had no obstacles in front of me?

(be as detailed and specific as possible)

Complete this sentence:

"Once my desired state is manifested (as described above in this area of life), the following will be possible for me:

What is getting in the way of me having this desired state right now in this area of my life?

List as many tangible hurdles that are in the way right now:

i.e. professional credentials, specific equipment, or physical requirements.

List as many intangible hurdles that are in the way right now:

i.e. fears, inner criticism, and other beliefs that limit you

What am I willing to give up in order to pursue the desired state?

i.e. time, comfort, convenience, money

Who do I trust to hold me accountable right now if I share my intentions to take action toward getting what I want in this area of my life?

Name_____

In what way would I want to be held accountable by this person − i.e. check in with me once a week? Once a month? Or 6 months from today? Phone calls, emails, in person visits?

Intention Statement: Fill in the blanks:

As of today (INSERT DATE), I commit to taking the following 3 action steps toward manifesting my desired state in this area of my life:

1.

2.

3.

I will ask (INSERT NAME) to be my accountability coach in this endeavor by opening up to (INSERT DAILY, WEEKLY, MONTHLY) check in (CALLS/EMAILS) until I accomplish these tasks.

Having worked through these journal points, what bubbles up in your mind? *What seems possible that didn't seem possible before? How would you describe your energy level right now? What fears or obstacles continue to seem daunting? What fears or obstacles have diminished a bit?*

Attitude
Put it Back
Assignment

Below are suggestions specific to this message that are recommended to continue your personal work on this topic. The Exercise sheets (Tool Kit) and List of Books (Library) are located in Section V and VI in the back of the book.

<u>Exercises</u>

Productize You

Books for Life

<u>Books</u>

Truman

Well Being

9 Things A Leader Must Do

Outliers

The Help

Notes

Attitude
Message 3

<u>More Room to Sit</u>

'Sometimes the best gain is to lose'
George Herbert

I recently stepped down from a volunteer position that has been a passionate outlet for my desire to guide, educate, and inspire young people for a number of years. While I knew the time was right to step down, what I didn't fully anticipate was the sense of loss that would accompany my decision to step away from this role.

And as I have experienced with other losses in my life, there's a disconcerting *empty spot* that is calling for my attention.

Loss of any role brings about a disruption in our sense of place or position, regardless of whether the loss is by choice or by circumstance. That empty spot can emerge from situations such as: the loss of a job, a recasting of your career path, transitioning from one grade to the next in school, the loss of a life partnership, or the stepping back from a previously held ideal that no longer seems to fit.

What is clear to me is that these empty spots can be places of great opportunity, while at the same time being sand traps to be navigated around.

If we're not mindful, those sand traps show up in the form of fears, inner criticism and other beliefs that limit you.

It is pretty easy to identify and, at times, dwell on what the loss has

removed from our life.

The more difficult, and arguably the more beneficial, thought-path to forge is the one that pursues answers to two fundamental questions:

1) What has this loss NOT changed?

and

2) What now becomes possible that wasn't before?

At 75 years of age, my grandmother endured the amputation of her right leg due to cancer. When she was out of surgery and able to receive visitors, I walked into her room trying my best not to stare at the empty spot in the bed where her leg used to be. But, my face must have shown how distracting the image was.

She reached for my hand, squeezed it tightly and said 'Come closer...now there's more room to sit and visit with me'.

I encourage you to look hard to see what your own empty spot has made more room for.

Attitude
More Room to Sit
Journal

What drew my attention to this message?

What is going on right now in my world that has caused this topic to resonate with me?

What do I want to make happen in my life (personal or professional) specific to this topic? What would be my desired state in this area of my life if I had no obstacles in front of me?

(be as detailed and specific as possible)

Complete this sentence:

"Once my desired state is manifested (as described above in this area of life), the following will be possible for me:

What is getting in the way of me having this desired state right now in this area of my life?

List as many tangible hurdles that are in the way right now:

i.e. professional credentials, specific equipment, or physical requirements.

List as many intangible hurdles that are in the way right now:

i.e. fears, inner criticism, and other beliefs that limit you

What am I willing to give up in order to pursue the desired state?

i.e. time, comfort, convenience, money

Who do I trust to hold me accountable right now if I share my intentions to take action toward getting what I want in this area of my life?

Name_____

In what way would I want to be held accountable by this person – i.e. check in with me once a week? Once a month? Or 6 months from today? Phone calls, emails, in person visits?

Intention Statement: Fill in the blanks:

As of today (INSERT DATE), I commit to taking the following 3 action steps toward manifesting my desired state in this area of my life:

1.

2.

3.

I will ask (INSERT NAME) to be my accountability coach in this endeavor by opening up to (INSERT DAILY, WEEKLY, MONTHLY) check in (CALLS/EMAILS) until I accomplish these tasks.

Having worked through these journal points, what bubbles up in your mind? *What seems possible that didn't seem possible before? How would you describe your energy level right now? What fears or obstacles continue to seem daunting? What fears or obstacles have diminished a bit?*

Attitude
More Room to Sit
Assignment

Below are suggestions specific to this message that are recommended to continue your personal work on this topic. The Exercise sheets (Tool Kit) and List of Books (Library) are located in Section V and VI in the back of the book.

Exercises

The Legacy Letter

Change Versus Transformation

The Wheel of Life

Books

Comfortable With Uncertainty

Necessary Endings

Notes

Attitude
Message 4

<u>Ditch the Wheels</u>

"It's not what you are that holds you back, it's what you think you're not."
Clarence Cresong

A common thought pattern that can emerge when faced with a challenge that you have no experience with or you feel 'out of your league' in navigating through often sounds something like:

"that's just NOT me' or 'I don't have the background to do...' or

'that would be too far of a stretch for me'.

A simple, but highly effective, coaching tool that often will break this pattern of thinking is called 'Ditch The Wheels' .

While the tool is built around the mastery of riding a bike without training wheels, if you haven't mastered that skill yet, you can easily substitute another childhood accomplishment of which you are personally proud

(i.e. learning to swim, drive a car, etc).

To start, simply ask yourself: 'When the desire to ditch the training wheels hit you, what did you do?'

Here was my own childhood approach:

1. I observed every bike rider on my street to try to understand what they were doing.

2. I asked my brother for tips and advice.

3. I practiced for 2 hours after school for weeks.

4. I asked my mom & dad to watch me.

5. I promised myself a set of tricked out handle-bars as a reward once I made my goal.

Looking for clues above that can be re-purposed and applied to whatever current goal or challenge you are facing, the proven approach could be re-stated as follows: .

1. Identify and observe experts in the field for form, technique, and style.

2. Seek advice from a mentor.

3. Invest the time to practice on your own.

4. Enlist the support of a loved one as you tackle this new endeavor.

5. Establish an incentive to keep your motivation high.

So, if you're caught right now in thought patterns around what you are NOT....

think about getting those training wheels off and follow your own five-step process.

Attitude
Ditch the Wheels
Journal

What drew my attention to this message?

What is going on right now in my world that has caused this topic to resonate with me?

What do I want to make happen in my life (personal or professional) specific to this topic? What would be my desired state in this area of my life if I had no obstacles in front of me?

(be as detailed and specific as possible)

Complete this sentence:

"Once my desired state is manifested (as described above in this area of life), the following will be possible for me:

What is getting in the way of me having this desired state right now in this area of my life?

List as many tangible hurdles that are in the way right now:

i.e. professional credentials, specific equipment, or physical requirements.

List as many intangible hurdles that are in the way right now:

i.e. fears, inner criticism, and other beliefs that limit you

What am I willing to give up in order to pursue the desired state?

i.e. time, comfort, convenience, money

Who do I trust to hold me accountable right now if I share my intentions to take action toward getting what I want in this area of my life?

Name_____

In what way would I want to be held accountable by this person – i.e. check in with me once a week? Once a month? Or 6 months from today? Phone calls, emails, in person visits?

Intention Statement: Fill in the blanks:

As of today (INSERT DATE), I commit to taking the following 3 action steps toward manifesting my desired state in this area of my life:

1.

2.

3.

I will ask (INSERT NAME) to be my accountability coach in this endeavor by opening up to (INSERT DAILY, WEEKLY, MONTHLY) check in (CALLS/EMAILS) until I accomplish these tasks.

Having worked through these journal points, what bubbles up in your mind? *What seems possible that didn't seem possible before? How would you describe your energy level right now? What fears or obstacles continue to seem daunting? What fears or obstacles have diminished a bit?*

Attitude
Ditch the Wheels
Assignment

Below are suggestions specific to this message that are recommended to continue your personal work on this topic. The Exercise sheets (Tool Kit) and List of Books (Library) are located in Section V and VI in the back of the book.

<u>Exercises</u>

Know This

Productize You

Choose a Wolf

<u>Books</u>

What Should I Do With My Life?

The Power of Self Coaching

Strengths Finder 2.0

Notes

Attitude
Message 5

<u>Where is the Fun?</u>

People rarely succeed unless they have fun in what they are doing. – Dale Carnegie

What do you have planned for today that fits
your own personal description of fun?

If the answer is 'nothing' or 'I don't know'.....why is that? What
rationale do you have that supports your acceptance of the fact
that on this day, you have not taken control of your day and pro-
actively planned to have some fun? Why is that OK for you?

Recently, I did something slightly self-indulgent involving the
purchase of a 'toy' that has 2 leather seats, 5 awesome speeds,
and ridiculously messes up my hair every time I use it.

In addition to it being a source of pure fun for me...I've noticed
something more: somewhere between 4th and 5th gear the seeds of
solutions to my challenging problems start to bubble up into my mind.

It's like the mental clutter is blown to the wind, and I can see things that are more evident when I'm in a 'fun' state of mind.

So, perhaps there's a coaching message here:

As we envelope ourselves in the responsibilities and pressures of our careers and family life, tending to this important activity falls lower and

lower on the priority list. We get wrapped up in the more noble 'to do' items which appear to have greater immediate results and serve some long-term value.

All animals, except humans, know that the principle business of life is to enjoy it.
– Samuel Butler

Try this:

For the next week, make the very last thing you do (work-related) each evening be a review of your schedule for the next day and identify where the FUN will be had.

Highlight it in a special font and begin anticipating it.

If you can't identify anything that will be fun for you, take the initiative to create something fun and put it on your schedule. Keep the commitment!

It doesn't have to be grand, over-the-top, all consuming things....it can be simple acts:

- Make a call to someone you love just to chat.

- Take your favorite client out for lunch.

- Grab a specialty coffee drink and read a tabloid magazine.

- Start writing that book that's waiting to be written.

Now, here's the guaranteed ROI

at least one of the following will be the result of your investment in fun that day:

You will get an immediate hit of anabolic, positive energy.

You will remember things about yourself that you like and enjoy.

Your mind will open up and blocked solutions to
your problems will appear as if by 'magic'.

And, listen to what the doctor says: *Fun is Good.*
– Dr. Seuss

Attitude
Where is the Fun?
Journal

What drew my attention to this message?

What is going on right now in my world that has caused this topic to resonate with me?

What do I want to make happen in my life (personal or professional) specific to this topic? What would be my desired state in this area of my life if I had no obstacles in front of me?

(be as detailed and specific as possible)

Complete this sentence:

"Once my desired state is manifested (as described above in this area of life), the following will be possible for me:

What is getting in the way of me having this desired state right now in this area of my life?

List as many tangible hurdles that are in the way right now:

i.e. professional credentials, specific equipment, or physical requirements.

List as many intangible hurdles that are in the way right now:

i.e. fears, inner criticism, and other beliefs that limit you

What am I willing to give up in order to pursue the desired state?

i.e. time, comfort, convenience, money

Who do I trust to hold me accountable right now if I share my intentions to take action toward getting what I want in this area of my life?

Name_____

In what way would I want to be held accountable by this person – i.e. check in with me once a week? Once a month? Or 6 months from today? Phone calls, emails, in person visits?

Intention Statement: Fill in the blanks:

As of today (INSERT DATE), I commit to taking the following 3 action steps toward manifesting my desired state in this area of my life:

1.

2.

3.

I will ask (INSERT NAME) to be my accountability coach in this endeavor by opening up to (INSERT DAILY, WEEKLY, MONTHLY) check in (CALLS/EMAILS) until I accomplish these tasks.

Having worked through these journal points, what bubbles up in your mind? *What seems possible that didn't seem possible before? How would you describe your energy level right now? What fears or obstacles continue to seem daunting? What fears or obstacles have diminished a bit?*

Attitude
Where is the Fun?
Assignment

Below are suggestions specific to this message that are recommended to continue your personal work on this topic. The Exercise sheets (Tool Kit) and List of Books (Library) are located in Section V and VI in the

back of the book.

Exercises

Wheel of Life

The Miracle Exercise

Books

When You Are Engulfed In Flames

The World According to Garp

A Prayer for Owen Meany

Notes

_____

_____

_____

_____

_____

_____

_____

_____

_____

_____

_____

_____

_____

_____

_____

_____

_____

_____

_____

_____

_____

_____

_____

_____

_____

_____

_____

_____

Attitude
Message 6

<u>One Cup Rule</u>

Hurricane Sandy hit my hometown pretty ferociously this past week. After a harrowing night of fierce winds and rain, I ventured out in the early morning hours by car to check out the area damage and try to find a first cup of coffee from anyone

who hadn't lost power.

The coffee cart located inside one local supermarket was the only place functioning with a generator. To my dismay, the line at the cart stretched 82 people strong looping around the produce section about 100 feet from the entrance.

I took my place in line at position #83.

I observed that the cart had one coffee urn operating from one brewing station. The urn served 20 cups of coffee. When the urn was empty, it took approximately 20 minutes to brew a fresh pot. You do the math and you'll get an idea of the time investment this was going to take.

As I watched the line move at a snail's pace, the most disturbing thing I saw was that some folks in line were taking up to 4 cups of coffee when it was there turn, for friends or family waiting at home. This had the ripple effect of making the line go even slower.

One courageous woman called out to the manager and made a pretty impassioned plea to institute a 'one cup' rule. Her position was that the only fair thing to do was to limit this precious commodity in the most equitable way possible in light of the extreme circumstances.

What followed her brave action was an uprising, of sorts. Those folks who were looking for more than one cup began a rather selfish argument displaying their sense of entitlement and disregard for the unique circumstances or for their fellow customers in line behind them.

One designer clad hot shot told the manager 'money is no object...I want what I want and I'll pay a premium for it if I have to'.

After a few minutes, the manager took a bold position that made a powerful statement about himself and his company.

'One cup rule for today', he said. 'For those who aren't happy with that, I respect your option to leave the line and find coffee elsewhere.'

To which, the 'money is no object' fellow left the store in a huff, got into his Range Rover and drove off likely not to bring his loafers back into this store for quite some time to come. As for me, he's got a customer for life.

Two leadership heroes in this post-Sandy scene:

The woman who had the courage to stand up for her beliefs, eloquently express her position in a manner that was respectful of the greater good for all in a unique situation that called for some level of shared selflessness.

The manager who understood that circumstances dictated unique actions that were not going to please everyone, rather than avoid making a tough decision - he made one.

I got my coffee just 43 minutes later.

Attitude
One Cup Rule
Journal

What drew my attention to this message?

What is going on right now in my world that has caused this topic to resonate with me?

What do I want to make happen in my life (personal or professional) specific to this topic? What would be my desired state in this area of my life if I had no obstacles in front of me?

(be as detailed and specific as possible)

Complete this sentence:

"Once my desired state is manifested (as described above in this area of life), the following will be possible for me:

What is getting in the way of me having this desired state right now in this area of my life?

List as many tangible hurdles that are in the way right now:

i.e. professional credentials, specific equipment, or physical requirements.

List as many intangible hurdles that are in the way right now:

i.e. fears, inner criticism, and other beliefs that limit you

What am I willing to give up in order to pursue the desired state?

i.e. time, comfort, convenience, money

Who do I trust to hold me accountable right now if I share my intentions to take action toward getting what I want in this area of my life?

Name_____

In what way would I want to be held accountable by this person — i.e. check in with me once a week? Once a month? Or 6 months from today? Phone calls, emails, in person visits?

Intention Statement: Fill in the blanks:

As of today (INSERT DATE), I commit to taking the following 3 action steps toward manifesting my desired state in this area of my life:

1.

2.

3.

I will ask (INSERT NAME) to be my accountability coach in this endeavor by opening up to (INSERT DAILY, WEEKLY, MONTHLY) check in (CALLS/EMAILS) until I accomplish these tasks.

Having worked through these journal points, what bubbles up in your mind? *What seems possible that didn't seem possible before? How would you describe your energy level right now? What fears or obstacles continue to seem daunting? What fears or obstacles have diminished a bit?*

Attitude
One Cup Rule
Assignment

Below are suggestions specific to this message that are recommended to continue your personal work on this topic. The Exercise sheets (Tool Kit) and List of Books (Library) are located in Section V and VI in the back of the book.

<u>Exercises</u>

Productize You

<u>Books</u>

Truman

The Good Life

Personal History

John Adams

The Greatest Generation

Notes

Leadership Foundation IV

INFLUENCE

Influence is the tangible and outward facing product of effective leadership. Rather than looking at leadership as an authoritative position or an organizational box, we are all well served to look at leadership as a 'position of influence' which we hold within our own world. This section brings to light personal levels of influence that go beyond a prescribed definition of leader to show in a personal way that we are ALL leaders with the potential to influence others more powerfully than we realize.

Influence
Thought Leadership

Once you've found your own voice, the choice to expand your influence, to increase your contribution, is the choice to inspire others to find their voice.
Stephen Covey

The challenge of leadership is to be strong, but not rude; be kind, but not weak; be bold, but not bully; be thoughtful, but not lazy; be humble, but not timid; be proud, but not arrogant; have humor, but without folly."
Jim Rohn

"Leadership is the capacity to translate vision into reality."
Warren Bennis

"The key to successful leadership today is influence, not authority."
Kenneth Blanchard

"Good leaders make people feel that they're at the very heart of things, not at the periphery. Everyone feels that he or she makes a difference to the success of the organization. When that happens, people feel centered and that gives their work meaning."
Warren Bennis

Great leaders are almost always great simplifiers, who can cut through argument, debate, and doubt to offer a solution everybody can understand."
General Colin Powel

Influence
Message 1

<u>The Future is Looking Bright, Son</u>

While boarding my flight home last week from a conference, I overheard

the end of a cell phone conversation.

The guy was about my age (young and vibrant)
and closed his conversation by saying:

'the future is looking bright, son...

I'll see you when I get home'.

In that moment, I was reminded of the countless conversations I had with
my dad in which he would assure me 'things will work out, you'll see...I
have faith in you'. If the conversations were in person, he'd put his hand
on the nape of my neck and give it a couple of gentle, but firm, squeezes.

And, in those moments, I would see what he saw...I would

KNOW that things would work out...and my faith in my own abilities would be restored and invigorated.

I vividly recall how, as if by magic, the insurmountable obstacles I had come to my father to discuss would transform into manageable challenges I grew energized to 'take on'.

In addition to my father, I have had the good fortune to have had a few bosses in my career that instilled that same level of inspiration at critical times on my professional path. As a result, those managers were the benefactors of some of my very best work, which delivered the kind of results that were a true reflection of their leadership talent.

As I flew home, the memories the conversation triggered made me think about two questions:

First, as a self-employed orphan now, who does this for me today in my life?

Where do I go to help me clear the mental clutter, distill my thoughts for clarity, and restore my confidence in my own strengths? What sage mentor have I cultivated in my life who will assure me that 'things will work out' or that 'the future is bright'?

Second, for whom in my life do I serve this purpose?

Who looks to me to help restore clarity? In what ways do I bring my clients, my colleagues, or my children to a place of remembering their own strengths? For whom does my own version of the 'gentle but firm neck-nape squeeze' instill a sense of peace and calm?

Ask yourself those questions. I encourage you to seek the answers especially if they don't come right away. We all lead, we all inspire, and we all have the power to bring out the best in someone closer to us than we think.

I'm pretty sure the guy telling his son 'the future is looking bright' at the Las Vegas airport last week, had no idea of the way in which he inspired me.

Influence
The Future is Looking Bright, Son
Journal

What drew my attention to this message?

What is going on right now in my world that has caused this topic to resonate with me?

What do I want to make happen in my life (personal or professional) specific to this topic? What would be my desired state in this area of my life if I had no obstacles in front of me?

(be as detailed and specific as possible)

Complete this sentence:

"Once my desired state is manifested (as described above in this area of life), the following will be possible for me:

What is getting in the way of me having this desired state right now in this area of my life?

<u>List as many tangible hurdles that are in the way right now:</u>

i.e. professional credentials, specific equipment, or physical requirements.

<u>List as many intangible hurdles that are in the way right now:</u>

i.e. fears, inner criticism, and other beliefs that limit you

What am I willing to give up in order to pursue the desired state?

i.e. time, comfort, convenience, money

Who do I trust to hold me accountable right now if I share my intentions to take action toward getting what I want in this area of my life?

Name_____

In what way would I want to be held accountable by this person – i.e. check in with me once a week? Once a month? Or 6 months from today? Phone calls, emails, in person visits?

Intention Statement: Fill in the blanks:

As of today (INSERT DATE), I commit to taking the following 3 action steps toward manifesting my desired state in this area of my life:

1.

2.

3.

I will ask (INSERT NAME) to be my accountability coach in this endeavor by opening up to (INSERT DAILY, WEEKLY, MONTHLY) check in (CALLS/EMAILS) until I accomplish these tasks.

Having worked through these journal points, what bubbles up in your mind? *What seems possible that didn't seem possible before? How would you describe your energy level right now? What fears or obstacles continue to seem daunting? What fears or obstacles have diminished a bit?*

Influence
The Future is Looking Bright, Son
Assignment

Below are suggestions specific to this message that are recommended to continue your personal work on this topic. The Exercise sheets (Tool Kit) and List of Books (Library) are located in Section V and VI in the back of the book.

Exercises

The Miracle Exercise

The Legacy Letter

The Wheel of Life

Books

The Dream Manager

Letters to My Son

A Father's Love

Strong Fathers, Strong Daughters

Notes

_____
_____
_____
_____
_____
_____
_____
_____
_____
_____
_____
_____
_____
_____
_____
_____
_____
_____
_____
_____
_____
_____
_____
_____
_____
_____

Influence
Message 2

<u>Love on the Acela</u>

On a recent train ride heading to a client meeting, I took note of the guy sitting in the same row as me but opposite side of the aisle: Mid-20's , spikey and gelled 'just-out-of bed' hair, black Ray Ban style glasses, black t-shirt, jeans rolled up at the ankle, black converse sneakers (chuck taylor's) with no socks.

Got the visual?

Turns out that he was an Audio-Visual Production Manager, which became evident once he started up a phone conversation with a client. From the start of the discussion, it was clear that he had primary responsibility for handling the event on behalf of his company. I could tell the guy knew his stuff but it was his engaging and highly energetic confidence that drew me in to listen more intently to what he was saying.

Here's a few quotes from that conversation (yes, I took notes):

'I am so lucky to have you as my customer!'

'You are going to look TOTALLY Fly!"

'Are you as excited as me?'

'You have no idea how important you are to me!"

'I am sooo stoked!...Are you feeling the love?

'This is all about you - I'm just the co-pilot along for the ride. '

'I can and absolutely WANT to help you with that.'

'Anything I can do to make your life easier?'

'You are A.....MAZE.....ING!'

'Thank you so much....this has been awesome!
I can't wait to talk with you again. '

When the call ended, I had to fight the urge to
either start applauding or light a cigarette.

It was like, in the most professional sense of the word, this guy absolutely

made love to his client...right there on the Amtrak Acela Train 196.

It would be easy to dismiss the broad coaching applicability of this
story by citing the guy's youth or the less formal nature of the audio-
visual industry. But, I think that would be short sighted. This guy is
connected to a deeply personal passion that is impossible not to witness.
I felt enriched for having been an interloper and catching his energy
if only peripherally... I can only image what his clients must feel.

I want that....and I want to convey that.

Ask yourself these two questions using the name of one of your
most important stakeholders (client, boss, spouse, child):

1. When was the last time I made (FILL IN NAME) feel 'totally FLY'?

2. How would (FILL IN NAME) answer me if I asked 'do you have any idea how important you are to me?'.

If you're not sure of the answers, give (FILL IN NAME) a call and feel free to use any of the quotes above as conversation starters.

Influence
Love on the Acela
Journal

What drew my attention to this message?

What is going on right now in my world that has caused this topic to resonate with me?

What do I want to make happen in my life (personal or professional) specific to this topic? What would be my desired state in this area of my life if I had no obstacles in front of me?

(be as detailed and specific as possible)

Complete this sentence:

"Once my desired state is manifested (as described above in this area of life), the following will be possible for me:

What is getting in the way of me having this desired state right now in this area of my life?

List as many tangible hurdles that are in the way right now:

i.e. professional credentials, specific equipment, or physical requirements.

List as many intangible hurdles that are in the way right now:

i.e. fears, inner criticism, and other beliefs that limit you

What am I willing to give up in order to pursue the desired state?

i.e. time, comfort, convenience, money

Who do I trust to hold me accountable right now if I share my intentions to take action toward getting what I want in this area of my life?

Name_____

In what way would I want to be held accountable by this person – i.e. check in with me once a week? Once a month? Or 6 months from today? Phone calls, emails, in person visits?

Intention Statement: Fill in the blanks:

As of today (INSERT DATE), I commit to taking the following 3 action steps toward manifesting my desired state in this area of my life:

1.

2.

3.

I will ask (INSERT NAME) to be my accountability coach in this endeavor by opening up to (INSERT DAILY, WEEKLY, MONTHLY) check in (CALLS/EMAILS) until I accomplish these tasks.

Having worked through these journal points, what bubbles up in your mind? *What seems possible that didn't seem possible before? How would you describe your energy level right now? What fears or obstacles continue to seem daunting? What fears or obstacles have diminished a bit?*

Influence
Love on the Acela
Assignment

Below are suggestions specific to this message that are recommended to continue your personal work on this topic. The Exercise sheets (Tool Kit) and List of Books (Library) are located in Section V and VI in the back of the book.

<u>Exercises</u>

Productize You

Know This

Plug It In

<u>Books</u>

With Purpose

The Dream Manager

Mojo

The World According to Garp

Notes

Influence
Message 3

<u>The Right Question</u>

At a conference I attended recently, I sat through a sales presentation by a pretty reputable company delivered by a seemingly seasoned sales professional. After viewing a brief video overview of the company and its products, the sales guy asked me this question: 'What keeps you up at night?'.

Now, I know that this question is one that many of us have been taught to ask as a means of learning enough about a prospect to connect product benefits to pain points. But, in truth, this question has always been a pet peeve of mine.

As I see it, there are three ways to respond to that question:

I could actually tell the truth about what kinds of things keep me up at night. But unless the person asking is credentialed to prescribe Xanax, it would be quickly obvious that the asker is way out of his or her element.

I could respond with the obvious and rather scripted answer, which would include generic things like: Revenue, continued relevance, good health, etc. ...All of which will reveal nothing of any real value to the asker, but will keep the sales pitch going.

I could use this as a coaching moment to help this person 'up their game'.

Last week, I chose Number 3 by responding this way:

"You're asking the wrong question. What you should want to know from me is:

'what gets me out of bed in the morning?'.

If I tell you what keeps me up at night, you'll gain insight into my fears, my worries, and my regrets. I will be exposing my areas of vulnerability and I'm not ready to do that until I trust you.

If I tell you what gets me out of bed in the morning, you'll get to know what really drives me...where my passions lie. If you ask me about that, you're tapping into my sources of strength and optimism. You are allowing me to share my vision of the future which I enjoy talking about and will readily share.

Do you hear the subtle, yet profound, shift in that simple change to the question? Can you feel how much more 'possibility' oriented the right question can be?

Think about what becomes possible for your relationships if you found out the answer to that question from your most valued stakeholders... it could be game changing.

Ask yourself the question and see how revealing the answer is about what's really going on inside of you.

Be honest and allow the answer to open up some insight into what is driving you right now.

Influence
The Right Question
Journal

What drew my attention to this message?

What is going on right now in my world that has caused this topic to resonate with me?

What do I want to make happen in my life (personal or professional) specific to this topic? What would be my desired state in this area of my life if I had no obstacles in front of me?

(be as detailed and specific as possible)

Complete this sentence:

"Once my desired state is manifested (as described above in this area of life), the following will be possible for me:

What is getting in the way of me having this desired state right now in this area of my life?

List as many tangible hurdles that are in the way right now:

i.e. professional credentials, specific equipment, or physical requirements.

List as many intangible hurdles that are in the way right now:

i.e. fears, inner criticism, and other beliefs that limit you

What am I willing to give up in order to pursue the desired state?

i.e. time, comfort, convenience, money

Who do I trust to hold me accountable right now if I share my intentions to take action toward getting what I want in this area of my life?

Name_____

In what way would I want to be held accountable by this person – i.e. check in with me once a week? Once a month? Or 6 months from today? Phone calls, emails, in person visits?

Intention Statement: Fill in the blanks:

As of today (INSERT DATE), I commit to taking the following 3 action steps toward manifesting my desired state in this area of my life:

1.

2.

3.

I will ask (INSERT NAME) to be my accountability coach in this endeavor by opening up to (INSERT DAILY, WEEKLY, MONTHLY) check in (CALLS/EMAILS) until I accomplish these tasks.

Having worked through these journal points, what bubbles up in your mind? *What seems possible that didn't seem possible before? How would you describe your energy level right now? What fears or obstacles continue to seem daunting? What fears or obstacles have diminished a bit?*

Influence
The Right Question
Assignment

Below are suggestions specific to this message that are recommended to continue your personal work on this topic. The Exercise sheets (Tool Kit) and List of Books (Library) are located in Section V and VI in the back of the book.

Exercises

Know This

The Miracle Exercise

The Mala & the Mantra

Books

What Should I Do With My Life?

Well Being

Strengths Finder 2.0

Mojo

Notes

Influence
Message 4

<u>Just Two Questions</u>

My kids have told me I'm a telemarketer's worst nightmare.

The reason:

Before I allow the caller to launch into a scripted chat with me, I force him/her to answer two questions...

Who are you? What do you want?

(I am that blunt)

In a matter of seconds, I can make an intelligent decision about how to make use of my time right then. If the caller and his purpose are of relevance to me -

I'm all in, fully engaged.

165

If not...the call is over.

Sometimes, though, if the person's approach angers me, I'll tell the caller what he wants to hear and make him think he has a 'hot lead' when, in fact, this lead freezes the moment the phone is hung up.

There's an important leadership engagement lesson here:

Whether it's as overt as the telemarketer example or not, EVERYONE you come in contact with performs a similar screening process about you. Your ability to quickly and succinctly establish who you are and what you want will directly impact whether you get polite interaction, predictable and formulaic responses or full-on engagement.

Some of the most important work I do with clients who are seeking to 'amp up their game' is to help them with this very important foundation of self-awareness.

And while the answers to these questions require some degree of situational differentiation, the consistent key to showing up strong in this area of

self-leadership is to be succinct.

Less is definitely more.

Try this exercise:

1. Think about a relationship/partnership in your world that is either broken or not yielding its potential.

2. Clearly describe your specific role in the relationship.

3. Identify the way in which your organization (or situation) has empowered you to manage the relationship.

4. Articulate what a 'fixed' relationship/partnership

would look like.

Now, before you reach out to the person on the other side of the relationship,
spend some time developing your answers to these two questions, forcing

yourself to adhere to a five word limit:

Who are you *in five words or less?*

What do you want *in five words or less?*

A challenge I encourage you to stick with, because with time and practice,

it can quickly become one of your

strongest leadership engagement tools.

Influence
Just Two Questions
Journal

What drew my attention to this message?

What is going on right now in my world that has caused this topic to resonate with me?

What do I want to make happen in my life (personal or professional) specific to this topic? What would be my desired state in this area of my life if I had no obstacles in front of me?

(be as detailed and specific as possible)

Complete this sentence:

"Once my desired state is manifested (as described above in this area of life), the following will be possible for me:

What is getting in the way of me having this desired state right now in this area of my life?

List as many tangible hurdles that are in the way right now:

i.e. professional credentials, specific equipment, or physical requirements.

List as many intangible hurdles that are in the way right now:

i.e. fears, inner criticism, and other beliefs that limit you

What am I willing to give up in order to pursue the desired state?

i.e. time, comfort, convenience, money

Who do I trust to hold me accountable right now if I share my intentions to take action toward getting what I want in this area of my life?

Name_____

In what way would I want to be held accountable by this person – i.e. check in with me once a week? Once a month? Or 6 months from today? Phone calls, emails, in person visits?

Intention Statement: Fill in the blanks:

As of today (INSERT DATE), I commit to taking the following 3 action steps toward manifesting my desired state in this area of my life:

1.

2.

3.

I will ask (INSERT NAME) to be my accountability coach in this endeavor by opening up to (INSERT DAILY, WEEKLY, MONTHLY) check in (CALLS/EMAILS) until I accomplish these tasks.

Having worked through these journal points, what bubbles up in your mind? *What seems possible that didn't seem possible before? How would you describe your energy level right now? What fears or obstacles continue to seem daunting? What fears or obstacles have diminished a bit?*

Influence
Just Two Questions
Assignment

Below are suggestions specific to this message that are recommended to continue your personal work on this topic. The Exercise sheets (Tool Kit) and List of Books (Library) are located in Section V and VI in the back of the book.

<u>Exercises</u>

Books for Life

Productize You

Know This

<u>Books</u>

Personal History

Lindberg

Truman

John Adams

Notes

Influence
Message 5

<u>Celebrate Me Home</u>

We all have that one holiday song that seems to stir something inside of us, connecting us deeply to our higher selves.

For me, it's Kenny Loggins' rendition of *Please Celebrate Me Home*

I first heard this song my freshman year of college as I drove home for Thanksgiving break anticipating the pot of my grandmother's home made pierogies awaiting me on the stove.

Every year since then, it reminds me of just what a powerful source of strength and motivation my own 'celebrations home' have been.

Last week, as I heard the song on the radio for the first time this season, a fresh perspective hit me as I prepared to welcome home my college-age son for his freshman year Thanksgiving break.

Breaking apart the lyrics of the song opens up a leadership lesson that I believe we can all benefit from in terms of helping those that we lead manifest their best selves.

Whether we're welcoming our children home for a holiday break.....a veteran home from service abroad.......or, a professional road-warrior back from a grueling business trip......the power of 'celebrating someone home (or back to the office)' is all the same!

*

Please, celebrate me home...

a humble plea that asks to acknowledge the joy of reunion. A validation of connection - 'I'm home', 'I'm back', 'I'm here'

a declaration of presence that anticipates a reaction.

Come on and play my music.....

Remind that I do have a 'song' . Show me that my music is on the playlist here at home, or in the office.

Whenever I find myself too all alone,

I can sing me home...

There are times when the road gets tough...and I forget my own song. Remind me through celebration.

But, I'm bound to roam

As much as I love coming home, it's in my blood to roam. I know that. It's who I am and it's how I deliver my own personal value to the world.

Please Celebrate me home

Remind me of the greatness within me....

I need that.

*

Celebrating <u>anyone</u> home is leadership that honors the soul.

If you've ever been celebrated home....you get it.

If you're in a position to celebrate someone home....

you are blessed.

Honor that blessing.

Influence
Celebrate Me Home
Journal

What drew my attention to this message?

What is going on right now in my world that has caused this topic to resonate with me?

What do I want to make happen in my life (personal or professional) specific to this topic? What would be my desired state in this area of my life if I had no obstacles in front of me?

(be as detailed and specific as possible)

Complete this sentence:

"Once my desired state is manifested (as described above in this area of life), the following will be possible for me:

What is getting in the way of me having this desired state right now in this area of my life?

List as many tangible hurdles that are in the way right now:

i.e. professional credentials, specific equipment, or physical requirements.

List as many intangible hurdles that are in the way right now:

i.e. fears, inner criticism, and other beliefs that limit you

What am I willing to give up in order to pursue the desired state?

i.e. time, comfort, convenience, money

Who do I trust to hold me accountable right now if I share my intentions to take action toward getting what I want in this area of my life?

Name_____

In what way would I want to be held accountable by this person – i.e. check in with me once a week? Once a month? Or 6 months from today? Phone calls, emails, in person visits?

Intention Statement: Fill in the blanks:

As of today (INSERT DATE), I commit to taking the following 3 action steps toward manifesting my desired state in this area of my life:

1.

2.

3.

I will ask (INSERT NAME) to be my accountability coach in this endeavor by opening up to (INSERT DAILY, WEEKLY, MONTHLY) check in (CALLS/EMAILS) until I accomplish these tasks.

Having worked through these journal points, what bubbles up in your mind? *What seems possible that didn't seem possible before? How would you describe your energy level right now? What fears or obstacles continue to seem daunting? What fears or obstacles have diminished a bit?*

Influence
Celebrate Me Home
Assignment

Below are suggestions specific to this message that are recommended to continue your personal work on this topic. The Exercise sheets (Tool Kit) and List of Books (Library) are located in Section V and VI in the back of the book.

<u>Exercises</u>

Books for Life

Plug It In

The Legacy Letter

<u>Books</u>

The Dream Manager

Energy Leadership

9 Things A Leader Must Do

Notes

Influence
Message 6

<u>Change the Lesson</u>

'We teach people how to treat us'

Personal transformation of any kind is not for the faint of heart. It's tough... no matter if it's a job search, career change, or new personal status.

Transformation is deeper than change.

Sometimes, the most challenging roadblock to manifesting sustainable and effective transformation can be your personal relationship building style in place <u>prior</u> to your own transformation.

And, what served you well up to this point in creating a network of relationships, may become one of your most troublesome limitations.

If you are not mindful of the need to develop new self-leadership behaviors and techniques, you might easily slip into familiar patterns with both old and new relationships that exacerbate the roadblocks.

Why is this so tough? It requires a relocation outside of your behavioral comfort zone that is disruptive to your 'norm'. As the CEO of your own transformation, you are the teacher who must now teach those around you exactly how you are to be treated going forward.

Sounds grandiosely self-serving, I know, but if you don't take the pro-active lead on this who else will?

This is where we can all learn from effective leaders we have worked for, observed , or read about who have developed reputations for qualities such as being decisive, clear, focused, aware, engaged, and purposeful.

So, here are a few practical behavioral suggestions to help you begin to change the relationships around you to be more aligned with your desired transformation:

1. Know your value

2. Show your strengths

3. Say everything clearly

4. Pick up the phone

5. Leave nothing to interpretation

6. Stay on point

7. Shed all distractions

8. Guard your time

9. Interrupt the meeting

10. Make the decision

11. Say *no*, more often

12. Close some doors

13. Trust yourself more

14. Break the rules

If it is true that we teach people how to treat us...it's time to *change the lesson*.

Influence
Change the Lesson
Journal

What drew my attention to this message?

What is going on right now in my world that has caused this topic to resonate with me?

What do I want to make happen in my life (personal or professional) specific to this topic? What would be my desired state in this area of my life if I had no obstacles in front of me?

(be as detailed and specific as possible)

Complete this sentence:

"Once my desired state is manifested (as described above in this area of life), the following will be possible for me:

What is getting in the way of me having this desired state right now in this area of my life?

List as many tangible hurdles that are in the way right now:

i.e. professional credentials, specific equipment, or physical requirements.

List as many intangible hurdles that are in the way right now:

i.e. fears, inner criticism, and other beliefs that limit you

What am I willing to give up in order to pursue the desired state?

i.e. time, comfort, convenience, money

Who do I trust to hold me accountable right now if I share my intentions to take action toward getting what I want in this area of my life?

Name_____

In what way would I want to be held accountable by this person – i.e. check in with me once a week? Once a month? Or 6 months from today? Phone calls, emails, in person visits?

Intention Statement: Fill in the blanks:

As of today (INSERT DATE), I commit to taking the following 3 action steps toward manifesting my desired state in this area of my life:

1.

2.

3.

I will ask (INSERT NAME) to be my accountability coach in this endeavor by opening up to (INSERT DAILY, WEEKLY, MONTHLY) check in (CALLS/EMAILS) until I accomplish these tasks.

Having worked through these journal points, what bubbles up in your mind? *What seems possible that didn't seem possible before? How would you describe your energy level right now? What fears or obstacles continue to seem daunting? What fears or obstacles have diminished a bit?*

Influence
Change the Lesson
Assignment

Below are suggestions specific to this message that are recommended to continue your personal work on this topic. The Exercise sheets (Tool Kit) and List of Books (Library) are located in Section V and VI in the back of the book.

<u>Exercises</u>

Change versus Transformation

Know This

Plug It In

<u>Books</u>

The Saint, the Surfer, and the CEO

Necessary Endings

With Purpose

Notes

Section 5

The *Think About It* Library

Books in alphabetical order by Author's Last Name

The title, author, publisher, and a brief personal statement about all of the books which are recommended in the 'homework' section of each message is included in the library.

<u>Lindbergh</u>
by A. Scott Berg   G.P. Putnam's Sons

A complicated man who had vision, courage, and tenacity to accomplish more than what was thought humanly possible at the time he lived. -Not without his flaws, the complexity of his character and the way the author balances the information with insight is what makes him relatable and compelling.

What Should I Do With My Life?
by Po Bronson   Random House

Hot shot Silicon Valley guy shifts his own focus away from a lucrative finance career and becomes story-teller extraordinaire. A collection of mini-biographies about men and women who found their passion and then arranged their lives around it.....mid-way through their lives. Each story shows that we all face doubts, fears, and numbing acceptance of routine and then gives real-life examples of how others have figured out how to push through to take their lives in an entirely new direction.

The Greatest Generation
by Tom Brokaw   Random House

In many ways, the people in these stories are no different than any of us today, but the scope and magnitude of the times they lived in and the circumstances in which they served drive home the point that we are all capable of a whole lot more than we think we are.

Prayer, Faith, and Healing
by Kenneth Winston Caine
and Brian Paul Kaufman   Rodale Books

A book that is well worn, completely marked up, and very well loved in my personal library. It's broken down into sections that center around real life situations we have to deal with at some time or another and applies spiritual principles that help illuminate a path that can often look dark and scary. (Christian based)

Comfortable with Uncertainty
By Pema Chodron   Shambala Library

A collection of short teachings the can be piercing and,yet, comforting showing how moments (or times) of uncertainty are the placeholders for gifts to be examined. The author is a Buddhist nun who infuses deep spirituality into sometimes mundane fears that trip us up.

The Places That Scare You
by Pema Chodron   Shambala Library

Beyond uncertainty as in the previous book, the author offers a very grounded , yet spiritually based, approach to being fearless during the times when situations are paralyzing us into inaction. Concise and highly focused – this book is easy to read and one that becomes a convenient reference manual for working through your roadblocks.

Necessary Endings
by Dr. Henry Cloud   Harber Business

This guy has written many very well regarded business books. The subject matter of this one grabbed my attention from the title through the last page. He pokes deeply at the notion that progress requires *endings*, some of which are highly painful and emotion-filled and others which are freeing and energizing. He gives the reader usable and effective tools for managing the process of continuously handling the necessary endings we face all the time as we move toward our goals, both personal and professional.

9 Things a Leader Must Do
by Dr. Henry Cloud   Thomas Nelson

Easy to read, logical in it's simplicity, and take-aways that you'll likely use from the first time you pick up the book. For me, it validated things I knew and also showed me areas where my energy would be better served and give me a better return on the investment.

The Sedona Method
by Hale Dwoskin   Sedona Press

I won't lie – it wasn't until reading this a second time that it completely connected with me. A little bit intense and prone to a slightly 'new age-y' approach, this book is rich in content. At its core, the book is about releasing old thought patterns that are getting in your way today. It shows the reader how to confront, understand, and aggressively dismiss those old patterns that don't work any longer. If you choose to read it…I encourage you to push through it as I believe the gems are there to discover and worth the work to read.

With Purpose
by Ken Dychtwald   Collins Living

What happens once you're wildly successful in your career, have achieved the goals you've set for yourself, and you're only at mid-life? This book explores the mindset of folks who have hit the mid point and are now shifting from success to purpose. What intrigued me about this book was that regardless of outward success levels, the personal challenges to finding and living with purpose are the same for everyone. This is a great read and one that tapped deeply into my own sense of purpose.

Outliers
by Malcolm Gladwell   Little Brown

Through the stories and Gladwell's philosophy about the role of 'parentage and patronage' on success, this book opened me up to release my own limiting belief that highly successful people are somewhat 'different' than me. He has a very readable style of writing and his stories reveal the commonalities we share and don't share with the likes of Michael Jordan and Bill Gates. This book made me challenge my own notion of how my GAIL's have impacted my approach to business and life.

A Father's Love
by David Goldman   Viking

This guy went through hell getting his son back in a custody battle that was fought between family courts in the US and Brazil, after his estranged wife deceptively took the boy to visit his Brazilian grandparents. The story made the news for a few years as he navigated incredibly complicated international custody and cultural challenges. The writing style is a little bit one-sided, but it doesn't diminish the story of this guy living out his purpose and not backing down from any obstacles in pursuit of his goal. It's inspirational at many levels.

Mojo
by Marshall Goldsmith   Hyperion

Easy to read, relatively straight forward concepts, and packaged in a way that delivers the kind of boost to help you get back on your professional game. Lots of easy to reference ideas that can be put into action immediately.

The Good Life
by Peter. J. Gomes   Harper

A highly spiritual book that examines the concept of what a good life is and how does one actually create it. Christian-based philosophies that present the material in a way that causes the reader to examine his or her own motives to better understand what is driving us. It helps you answer the questions: Who am I? and What do I want?

Personal History
by Katherine Graham   Vintage

What captivated me about this autobiography was how completely candid and vulnerable Mrs.

Graham made herself in this book. Strip away the outward advantages and gifts her life was filled with, and I came to see the human story of a person who's life did not go in the direction she ever intended it nor expected it to go. There's a very compelling simplicity with which she processed, accepted, and then embraced the new direction her life would take her. There's a lesson in this book about taking that curve in the road and tearing it up.

The World According to Garp
by John Irving   Simon & Schuster

Jenny Garp is a woman who is resolute in who she is and accepts not a single obstacle in her way to reach her goal. In the middle of Irving's typical collection of odd characters and outrageous plotlines, you see Jenny emerge with a strength and clarity of purpose that can only be described as 'driven'. A fun book to read with a lead character to learn leadership skills from.

A Prayer for Owen Meany
by John Irving   Morrow

Classic Irving story-telling style mixing eclectic characters with multi-layered story lines, this novel brings to life a little guy who might not know exactly what his purpose is in life but is absolutely sure he has one. You can't not root for this guy or help but admire his tenacity in looking for and being open to find his true purpose in life.

The Dream Manager
by Matthew Kelly   Beacon Publishing

A business fable that is a quick and easy read. Simply put, if you want the most out of the people you lead…know THEIR dreams. Help them achieve THEIR dreams through their work with you. This books shifts the outdated question of "What's in it for you" to a deeper and more empowering quest for a manager to know about his team members: "What are you in it for?".

The Power of Self Coaching
by Joseph J. Luciani, Ph.D.   Wiley

This book presents a basic Five-Step plan to lay the groundwork for moving ahead in life or your career. The book contains many self-reflective exercises that do a good job in bringing internal obstacles to light and provide insight into conquering them.

Truman
by David McCullough   Simon & Schuster

Admittedly, I'm a biography junkie..., so my bias will come through in choosing this book. I suggest you read this only if you can put political persuasion aside and I hope that you will come to see Truman as a guy with an iron-clad sense of greater purpose who was also riddled with deep fears and insecurities about his capabilities. Throughout all his challenges...he pushed on, he kept to his priorities, and he remained as true to his baseline principles as he could.

John Adams
by David McCullough   Simon & Schuster

Similar to Truman, what I like about this book is its balanced portrayal of a complicated man who lived through a very complicated time in history. Consistently through the book, what unfolds is an authentic man who lived by his principles and appeared to do his best to stick to them for the long haul. It's a great story about knowing yourself well enough to exert influence without compromising self.

Strong Fathers, Strong Daughters
by Meg Meeker, M.D.   Ballantine Books

This is a fantastic book that explores the powerful ways in which fathers influence the way their daughters see the world. The book points to ten 'secrets every father should know'....they are not so much a secret as they are fundamental ways of being that profoundly shape our daughters' lives and the way they will interact with their world. This book forces the reader to get familiar and honest with his truest parenting (and leadership) principles.

Letters to My Son
by Kent Nerburn   New World Library

I wish I had written his book. The sub title says it all: 'A Father's Wisdom on Manhood, Women, Life, and Love'. A topical letter of love written by a man to his son imparting the kind of perspective and guidance that can only come from the father's life lived with fearless purpose.

Strengths Finder 2.0
by Tom Rath   Gallup Press

This book comes with login credentials to take an online assessment designed to help you identify and validate your Top Five Talents. Once you take the assessment, your results are emailed to you and the book helps guide you in understanding the ways in which your own unique Top 5 can guide you in looking at career selection or advancement.

Well Being
by Tom Rath, Jim Harter   Gallup Press

Written from a business person's perspective, this book breaks down the concept of 'well being' into five key categories: Career, Social, Financial, Physical, and Community. The writers then provide the reader with tools, exercises, data, and insights on how to maximize a sense of well being in each category.

Energy Leadership
by Bruce D Schneider   John Wiley & Sons

An engaging account (which is a compilation of actual client situations) of an organizational shift toward anabolic (constructive, enhancing) energy and its impact on bottom line results. This book explains the concepts and skills involved in leading one's own energy and the energy of others. Easy to read, the book provides tangible examples which can impact one's organization, and indeed, one's life.

When You are Engulfed in Flames
by David Sedaris   Little Brown

Just plain fun. A delightful diversion from whatever is causing you stress. In fact, just about anything written by this guy will make you laugh out loud.

The Saint, the Surfer, and the CEO
by Robin Sharma   Hay House

A rich and deeply textured story about living your heart's desire. Centering on a guy at mid life who's questioning what's next for himself, the core message of the book is delivered by three profoundly impactful sages who come into the lead character's life at a time when he feels 'stuck'. We can all relate to this story. And the message from each sage brings a powerful and distinct message that touched me deeply.

The Help
by Kathryn Stockett   Putnam

Simply put, this book is about doing the right thing…regardless of risk or result. Each in his and her own way, the primary characters of this work of fiction reveal the turmoil that accompanies the decision to do the right thing. We can all learn from this book.

The Simple Feeling of Being
by Ken Wilber   Shambhala

Presented with strong Buddhist philosophies, the author pushes the reader to get to the underlying 'self' that we all must get to know if we ever hope to live a fulfilling and purposeful life. This book is a compilation of writings from the author put together in a very practical and readable way.

THE *Think About It* TOOL KIT

EXERCISES DESIGNED TO MOVE YOU FROM THOUGHT TO ACTION

The following self-coaching exercises and readings are to be used in conjunction with the specific recommendations provided after each topical coaching message in this book.

List of Exercises (details on the following pages)

1. Know This

2. Books for Life

3. Change vs. Transformation

4. Choose a Wolf

5. Inner Blocks

6. Plug it In

7. Productize You

8. The Legacy Letter

9. The Mala & the Mantra

10. The Miracle Exercise

11. The Peasant & Zemyne

12. The Wheel of Life

KNOW THIS

Exercise

Above all else, to be an effective leader, you must be able to articulate concise and clear answers to these two questions: <u>Who are you? What do you do?</u> . In order to begin to bring clarity for you, the following exercise breaks down each question into four steps:

<u>Question #1: Who are you?</u>

Step 1:

Name your top three personal attributes/strengths/talents. (Adjectives)

i.e. Smart, Disciplined, Articulate, Experienced

Step 2:

Prioritize them in order of most prominence and consistency that people you engage with experience when they interact with you. If you are unsure, validate this with a few trusted personal mentors. Select the ONE single attribute that you feel most connected to and reflects your most powerful personal imprint you bring to your position. Select the ONE that no one can refute about you! Be bold!

i.e. Disciplined

Step 3:

Articulate the position you hold, or strive to hold, in functional terms.

i.e. a Vice President of Sales is a 'leader of the sales organization'.

a Director of Customer Care is a 'driver of client satisfaction'.

Step 4:

Put it together:

Who am I?

I am a smart leader of the sales organization.

I am a disciplined driver of client satisfaction.

Question #2: What do I do?

Step 1:

Name the top three accountabilities your position has to the organization. (Nouns)

If you are unsure, look over your job description and pull specific deliverables from there.

i.e. new customer acquisition, client retention

Step 2:

Identify the single most important accountability that directly ties to the organization's achievement of its mission. You must reduce this down to one single deliverable that can be directly tied to the company's purpose.

i.e. revenue, happy clients

Step 3:

Name your key stakeholder for the position you hold. This can be the organization, at large, or can be a specific title-holder within the organization depending on your specific position.

i.e. CEO, Shareholders, Executive Committee, Fellow Employees

Step 4:

Put it all together:

What do I do?

I deliver new customer revenue streams to support the Company's strategic mission and objectives.

or

I keep clients happy thereby giving my organization a steady stream of predictable, repeatable revenue.

BOOKS FOR LIFE

Exercise

In this exercise, think about one book that has touched you deeply enough that you carry its impact inside of you for month or years after first reading it. To help you gain insight into that connection to the story, answer the following questions about the book.

Name of Book:

Author:

Year you first read the book:

Year(s) of subsequent readings of the book:

What is the central theme of the book?

Who are the heroes?

Who are the villains?

What obstacles were overcome by the main hero?

What attribute(s) does the hero have that allowed him or her to overcome the obstacles?

What characteristics do you share with any of the characters?

If you could re-write the story to suit your own personal viewpoint, how might you change it?

If you have re-read the book more than once, what new insights have you had that you didn't have after the first reading?

What primary core value of yours did the book serve as

validation of?

What primary belief about your self or the world did the book challenge?

Where do you keep the book? How often have you looked at it in the past 12 months? How often have you recommended it?

CHANGE VS. TRANSFORMATION

Exercise

Change fixes the past. Transformation creates the future.

The chances of getting what we want increase as we become clearer about what we want. Do you want a better version of now or something new? Both paths are difficult and produce rewards. Choose wisely.

CHANGE requires becoming familiar with the current situation, and working to make things better, faster, cheaper, or some other "er" word. The past is the fundamental reference point and actions are intended to alter what already happened. The success of a CHANGE initiative is judged by efficiencies and economies that are realized at the end of our effort, compared with when you started. When you choose CHANGE, your future is really a reconditioned or improved version of the past.

TRANSFORMATION is an assertion that our actions today create our future tomorrow. The future can be described and realized when you free yourself from constraints of the past. In transformation, you design your future and invent ways to bring it about. Transformation doesn't describe the future by referencing the past (better, faster, or cheaper); it births a future that is entirely new. Like CHANGE, TRANSFORMATION also begins with firmly grasping the current state of affairs — the *As Is* of the CORE PRIME. Without an intimate understanding of our *As Is*, we're delusional about the future from the outset. When you choose the path of TRANSFORMATION, it becomes easier to leave the past behind after thoroughly considering the *As Is*. You permit yourselves to envision the future freely; you make specific promises, with full INTEGRITY, about how things shall be. You take action to ensure that we live intoyour declarations about the future.

A butterfly is a transformation, not a better caterpillar.

Name the primary change you are seeking in your life today:

What will that change make possible for you that seems impossible today:

You will know that you have successfully changed when the following becomes visible and measurable to you:

Complete this sentence: With the change successfully implemented into my life, I will commit to the following three goals:

Answer this question for each goal listed above:

1. What will the accomplishment of this goal allow for you?

2. Who will be most directly impacted by your accomplishment of this goal?

3. What old thought patterns or habits will likely have to be released in order to achieve the goal?

4. What do you anticipate feeling when this goal is established?

Complete this sentence: My perception of people who have what I strive for already (my goal) is that they are different from me in the following way:

My perception of people who have what I strive for already (my goal) is that they are similar to me in the following way:

Name the transformation by assigning an attribute you will consciously embrace and own by completing this sentence: As a result of this transformation, I will use the following word or words to describe myself…i.e. disciplined, organized, accomplished. Use as many words as you feel appropriate to accurately define the transformation attributes you are striving for.

CHOOSE A WOLF

Reading

An old Cherokee is teaching his grandson about life.

"A fight is going on inside me," he said to the boy.

"It is a terrible fight and it is between two wolves. One is evil - he is anger, envy, sorrow, regret, greed, arrogance, self-pity, guilt, resentment, inferiority, lies, false pride, superiority, and ego."

He continued, "The other is good - he is joy, peace, love, hope, serenity, humility, kindness, benevolence, empathy, generosity, truth, compassion, and faith. The same fight is going on inside you - and inside every other person, too."

The grandson thought about it for a minute and then asked his grandfather,

"Which wolf will win?"

The old Cherokee simply replied,

"The one you feed."

INNER BLOCKS

#1 GREMLIN: YOUR PERSONAL INNER CRITIC

Your inner critic that tells you, in one way or another, that you're not good enough.

'It's not what you are that holds you back, it's what you think you are not.'
Denis Waitley

#2 ASSUMPTIONS

An expectation that because something has happened in the past it will happen again.

'…man is so imprisoned in his type of thinking that he is simply incapable of fully understanding another standpoint'

Jung

#3 INTERPRETATIONS

An opinion or judgment that you create about an event, situation, person, or experience and believe to be true.

'We do not see the world as it is, we see it as we are'
Anais Nin

#4 LIMITING BELIEFS

Something that you accept about life, about yourself, about your world, or about the people in it, that limits you in some way. These beliefs are not fact based.

"Obstacles are those frightening things you see when you take your eye off the target"
Curt Carlson

* Reprinted with permission of Bruce D Schneider, Ph.D. of the Institute for Professional Excellence in Coaching (iPEC), May 2013

PLUG IT IN

Exercise

Plugging your goal into your higher power source

<u>Step 1: STATE YOUR GOAL:</u>

Example 1: To lose 30 pounds

Example 2: Achieve the position of Vice President

<u>Step 2: ARTICULATE THE REASON FOR YOUR GOAL:</u>

Example: I want to lose 30 pounds because it will make me feel better, look better, and be healthier.

Example 2: I want to achieve the position of Vice President because it will fulfill my desire for professional success and financial reward.

Step 3: IDENTIFY WHAT BECOMES POSSIBLE FOR YOU THROUGH ATTAINMENT OF THE GOAL:

Example 1: When I feel better, look better, and am healthier I am free from those distractions to be the best father, coach, and friend I am capable of being.

Example 2: With the fulfillment of professional success and financial reward, I can apply my talents toward creating new business opportunities that don't exist today.

Step 4: ESTABLISH HOW YOUR 'WHAT'S POSSIBLE' WILL IMPACT THE WORLD:

Example 1: When I am the best father, coach, and friend I am capable of being, I can change the world by bringing out the best in those I love and serve.

Example 2: Through the creation of new business opportunities that don't exist today, I have the power to create new jobs that help to grow the economy.

Step 5: CONNECT YOUR IMPACT TO YOUR HIGHER PURPOSE:

Example 1: When I bring out the best in those I love and serve, I am a reflection of the universal love of God and I am living out my life's true purpose.

Example 2: By creating new jobs that grow the economy, I become a source of strength and positive change for the world, which is what my faith directs me to be.

Step 6: YOUR **PLUGGED IN GOAL**, REPHRASED:

Example 1: By shedding 30 distracting pounds I am carrying, I will be a reflection of the universal love of God through living out my true purpose.

Example 2: By becoming Vice President I will establish the foundation from which I will be a source of strength and positive change in the world.

Question:

In what ways will the re-phrased goal (step 6) help to bolster you this year when you might become distracted, discouraged, or energetically drained?

PRODUCTIZE YOU

Exercise

1. Imagine that you can magically be turned into a consumer product. What would you be?

    - When coming up with your answer, think about things like your purpose, your role, your strengths, you unique traits, and all that you bring to whatever job you undertake.

    - Try to connect a consumer product to the essence of what you do – not necessarily the functional task you perform.

    A few examples:

    -An <u>auditor</u> looks for things no one else can see – so, one product that fits could be an <u>X-Ray Machine</u>.

    - An <u>event planner</u> shields the attendee from any and all problems that might arise during an event – so, one product that fits could be an <u>umbrella.</u>

2. Decide your price point (high end, mid, or bargain) and explain why.

3. Where are you available for purchase (online? Nordstrom? Walmart?) and why?

4. What would be unique about your packaging (color? Material? Messaging?)

5. What kind of satisfaction guarantee would you come with?

THE LEGACY LETTER

Exercise

In this exercise, you are going to write a letter to someone important to you who is either one or two generations down the line from you - could be your child, your grandchild, or to a beloved niece or nephew.

The purpose of this exercise is to empower yourself to create a scenario whereby the path forward from this point is fully in your control. The intention behind the letter is to give you the opportunity to show your loved one a way to see past his or her own obstacles and grab hold of their dream.

In as much detail as you care to, take the time to show what it took to get you to the place of taking the first step toward what became a life-altering path. Share with your loved one what it was that allowed you to look at the obstacles that were in front of you (both external and internal) and take those important first, baby steps toward busting through them. Then, reveal to your loved one what those first steps (as terrifying as they might have seemed for you) eventually led you to.

Treat this Legacy Letter as the ultimate love letter to the next generation as a way to help them feel connected to you. This is also a chance for you to inspire your loved one in a way that shows how internal roadblocks (powerful as they can seem) are able to be conquered….as a way of saying, 'if I can do it, so can you'.

NOW, WRITE THE REST OF THE STORY FROM THIS DAY FORWARD. CREATE IN WORDS WHAT YOU WANT TO MAKE HAPPEN

THE MALA & THE MANTRA

Exercise

"Most of us spend too much time on what is urgent and not enough time on what is important."
- Stephen R Covey

Buddhist prayer beads (or 'malas') play a very important role in the spiritual life of many around the world. These traditional 'tools' are used to count the number of times a mantra is recited while meditating. Mantras are typically repeated hundreds or even thousands of times, and the 'mala' is used so that one can focus on the meaning of the mantra rather than counting its repetitions.

The 'mala' supports Covey's assertion above...focus on what is important (the meaning of the mantra) versus what might appear to be urgent.

So, what might you embrace as your personal 'mala'? What physical, tactile tool might you have at your disposal during the day to keep you attentive, and aware of staying focused on what is important versus what is simply urgent?

When choosing your 'mala', consider this: 1) Make is easy to access;

2) Make sure it nurtures a tactile pleasure; and 3) Select something that is uncomplicated.

Next, decide your mantra for the day, the week, the month, or the year - and commit to bringing it top of mind while using your 'mala'.

For this exercise, it might be useful to create a mantra that is based on one of your primary goals that you are focusing on with your personal coach. Keep the mantra concise (no more than 5 words) and powerfully positive:

i.e. I drive results –or- I lead with love –or- I AM the product

-or- I provide intelligence –or- My insight is wise

THE MIRACLE EXERCISE

Exercise

Read, think, ponder .....

Imagine that you have just awakened from a night's rest and whatever challenge you have come here with was miraculously overcome while you were sleeping. The challenge was completely solved overnight; but you were sleeping, and so you didn't know it was solved. You wake up and something is different. You inherently know that something is different, that something must have happened during the night. What is the first thing you notice that confirms that something actually did happen?

Now, in detail – using as much specificity as possible,
describe this day using all five senses:

How does it look? Your home? Your Office? Your car? Your back yard?

How does it smell? What scents are filling your space?

How does it sound? What do you hear? What don't you hear? What music is playing? What sounds are pervading your world?

How does it feel? What are you wearing? What furnishings are surrounding you? What type of energy do you have? What inspirations are manifesting?

How does it taste? What food is in your refrigerator? What entrée's are served to you? What does your fully stocked pantry include?

Who is around you? Who is NOT around you? What people are playing a prominent role in your life? What people are playing a minor role in our life?

What insight do you have that you didn't have the night before?

* *This exercise reprinted with permission of the Institute for Professional Excellence in Coaching (iPEC), May 2013*

THE PEASANT & ZEMYNE

Reading

Zemyne was once a lovely girl who refused the advances of a wicked magician. He cursed her and she assumed her present form, that of an ugly and poisonous serpent. Whoever wishes to rescue her must beat her until her skin falls off. Then he must burn the skin immediately, to prevent her from resuming her present form.

A young peasant habitually killed all the snakes he found in the garden, forest, and field. One day, he was cutting grass in the meadow when he suddenly heard a loud hiss. He became aware of a movement in the grass behind him. Looking around, he recognized Zemyne and he had often dreamed of rescuing the maiden.

Seeing his chance, the peasant pinned the snake's head against the earth with the blade of his sickle. Then he grabbed a knotted branch with his free hand and pounded the snake furiously until the skin broke open. All of a sudden a beautiful maiden was standing in front of him. Beside her sparkled the skin, now a beautiful, multi-colored dress.

The maiden reached for the dress, but the peasant was faster. He grabbed the garment, put it beneath his arm, and led the maiden to his home. There he gave her new clothes and food. She smiled charmingly and said nothing of her past life.

They married and lived happily together for many years. The wife gave her husband many children, and their joy increased still more. But, one day, the wife found a chest containing the multi-colored dress, for the peasant, instead of burning it,

had hidden it away.

She put it on and immediately changed back into a snake. Then she killed her husband and children with her poisonous bite and, leaving the farmstead, took up her old residence in the meadow by the woods.

The point:

BURN THE DRESS!

THE WHEEL OF LIFE

Exercise

THE WHEEL OF LIFE
Exercise

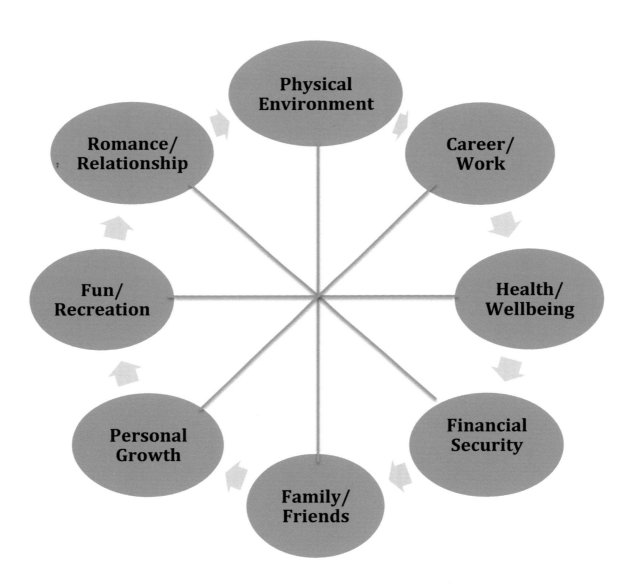

Rate your personal level of satisfaction in each of the spokes of the wheel.
Connect the dots and see where the bumps and valleys are in own wheel.

Pay close attention to those areas that got the highest and lowest rankings.

Be a voice, not an echo